The Dead Sleep Lightly

The Dead Sleep Lightly

JOHN DICKSON CARR

*Edited and with an Introduction
by Douglas G. Greene*

PUBLISHED FOR THE CRIME CLUB BY
DOUBLEDAY & COMPANY, INC.
GARDEN CITY, NEW YORK
1983

ACKNOWLEDGMENTS

In addition to those whom I acknowledged in an earlier John Dickson Carr collection, *The Door to Doom*, I should like to express my gratitude to the following for their enthusiasm, encouragement, and assistance: Rosalie Abrahams, Dana Batory, Peter Blau, Christianna Brand, Jon Breen, Wooda N. Carr II, Michael Cook, Paul Crane, Edward Delafield, Lillian de la Torre, Elizabeth Ferrars, Alan Ferris of the British Broadcasting Corporation, Benjamin Fisher, Philip Flynn, the late James Haff, John Hagan, Howard Haycraft, James Keirans, Roger Kuehl, Steve Lewis, Bill Loeser, John McAleer, Michael McVaugh, the late Ngaio Marsh, Gladys Mitchell, Paul Moy, Otto Penzler, Barry Pike, Bill Pronzini, Hugh Rawson, John Reynolds, Larry Rickert, Charles Shibuk, David Siegel, Peter and Paula Sperling, Peter Stern, Charles Van Wissink, William Willcox, and Adrienne Williams. Thanks also go to Terrence Rafferty and the staff of Doubleday & Company for shepherding this book through the press. I owe an especial debt of gratitude to John R. Young.

DGG

Library of Congress Cataloging in Publication Data

Carr, John Dickson, 1906–1977.
  The dead sleep lightly.

  (Crime club)
  Contents: The black minute—The Devil's saint—
The dragon in the pool—[etc.]
  1. Detective and mystery plays, American.
2. Radio plays, American. I. Greene, Douglas G.
II. Title.
PS3505.A763D35 1983   812'.52
ISBN 0-385-18714-9
Library of Congress Catalog Card Number 82-45870

Contents

INTRODUCTION: *John Dickson Carr and the Radio Mystery* by Douglas G. Greene   1

The Black Minute   13

The Devil's Saint   35

The Dragon in the Pool   53

The Dead Sleep Lightly   71

Death Has Four Faces   97

Vampire Tower   113

The Devil's Manuscript   131

White Tiger Passage   147

The Villa of the Damned   165

Introduction

JOHN DICKSON CARR AND
THE RADIO MYSTERY

The Golden Age of the detective novel and the Golden Age of radio drama came together in the late 1930s and the early 1940s. The detective novel matured between the two world wars when Agatha Christie, Dorothy L. Sayers, Ellery Queen, and others produced elaborate entertainments with corpses found in bizarre circumstances, and with eccentric detectives who solved crimes by fingering the least likely suspects. By the late 1920s, the rule had been firmly established that detective stories had to "play fair"; all the clues available to the detective had to be given to the reader. The detective story was thus a challenge between the author and the reader; it was, in John Dickson Carr's famous phrase, "the grandest game in the world."

Radio drama came of age, both in Britain and America, a bit later. Although radio plays first appeared in the late 1920s, it was not until a few years later that the Shadow and Sherlock Holmes, the Lone Ranger and Fu Manchu began their careers on the radio. During the 1940s, important mystery writers like Sayers, Queen, Cornell Woolrich, and Anthony Boucher were writing for the radio. But perhaps the key year was 1939: that was when John Dickson Carr, who was later to be proclaimed by the Mystery Writers of America as a Grand Master, wrote his first radio drama.

Carr was then thirty-three years old, and during his nine years as a professional writer he had some thirty detective novels to his credit. After a childhood in Pennsylvania (his father had been a congressman), Carr had moved to England in 1932. The land of Sherlock Holmes and Father Brown and Fu Manchu's nemesis, Nayland Smith, seemed to Carr not only the natural home for a detective novelist, but also the ideal place to write stories emphasizing the continuing values of the past—romance, fair play, and honor.

After first writing about a flamboyant French detective named Henri Bencolin, Carr began two series of novels featuring English detectives. Sir Henry Merrivale, whose cases Carr recounted under the pseudonym of "Carter Dickson," was originally a composite of several people, but as the Second World War approached and Carr came to admire the pugnacious, never-say-die facet of the British character, Merrivale picked up some of Winston Churchill's public personality. Carr never wrote about Merrivale for the radio, but his other major detective, Dr. Gideon Fell, appears in several plays. Fell was based on the appearance and mannerisms of G. K. Chesterton, whose classic Father Brown stories influenced Carr even more than did A. Conan Doyle's Sherlock Holmes.

Several of Carr's early novels set in England are told from the viewpoint of various American travelers who represent Carr's fascination with the standards and patterns of English life. Although his characters, especially Merrivale, have an American penchant for slang, his settings in pubs, country houses, and London clubs represent the British detective novel of the 1930s. Kingsley Amis recently remarked that Carr "developed a feeling for the nuances of local life sometimes denied grander writers, and his ear for English turns of phrase, though not quite infallible, is unsurpassed by any other foreign-born writer known to me." So British were his works that American critics suggested that the name "John Dickson Carr" was the alter ego of a British writer. One reviewer, impressed by the humor and tight plotting of his Merrivale novels, claimed that the books were actually written by P. G. Wodehouse. Just as fantastic was the suggestion, based on the shuddery atmosphere of some of the Dr. Fell stories, that "Carr" and "Carter Dickson" were both pseudonyms of the British occultist Montague Summers.

Carr took these attributions of his works in good-humored resignation, but behind such speculation was the truth that Carr was able to combine comedy and spookiness in a way that, book by book, might be Wodehouseian or occultist, but was at base a Carrian synthesis. Only one of his comic plays is included in this volume; most of the others are neo-Gothic in mood. Unlike many of his contemporaries who consciously avoided atmosphere in their detective novels, Carr reveled in it. He spent longer investigating the background of his tales than he did in the actual writing. He visited manor houses, examined watches in the shape of skulls, and read about lurid practices of the past, not only to describe such things in convincing detail but also to absorb the feelings that they arouse. In his stories, atmosphere becomes (in a favorite word in his early works) palpable.

Carr's use of atmosphere is key to his combination of rational detection with seemingly supernatural events. He uses setting and mood to make the reader expect the supernatural and thus misdirect him from the clues that eventually lead to a rational solution. Carr was as interested in describing the creaking of a door and the wind whistling about the eaves as he was in the crime itself; the trappings are as significant as the events. Dr. Fell and Carr's other investigators find crime against a background of ancient legends and modern witchcraft. And the murder is part of this mood of brooding terror, for it seems that no human being can have been responsible. In his novels, short stories, and plays, Carr invented about one hundred different ways of committing apparently impossible crimes. He was master of the locked-room murder in which the victim is stabbed or poisoned or shot in what seems a completely inaccessible room. Carr could also have people disappear in equally impossible circumstances; indeed his first detective story, published while he was still in college, demonstrates how a man can vanish from a guarded chamber and then reappear within a locked building. Carr provided rational explanations to such "miracle crimes" without recourse to secret passages or other hoary devices.

Carr's model for impossible crimes as well as for plot development was the work of G. K. Chesterton. With the publication of the second Gideon Fell novel, Dorothy Sayers recognized that the detective was based on Chesterton and the story-telling itself was derived from the creator of Father Brown:

> Chestertonian also are the touches of extravagance in character, and the sensitiveness to symbolism, to historical association, to the shapes and colours of material things, to the crazy terror of the incongruous. Mr. Carr can lead us away from the small, artificial, brightly-lit stage of the ordinary detective plot into the menace of outer darkness. He can

create atmosphere with an adjective, and make a picture from a wet iron railing, a dusty table, a gas-lamp blurred by the fog. He can alarm with an allusion or delight with a rollicking absurdity—in short, he can write—not merely in the negative sense of observing the rules of syntax, but in the sense that every sentence gives a thrill of positive pleasure.

To create mood by suggestion, to lead his audience into the menace of outer darkness—these are Carr's qualities both as a novelist and as a radio dramatist.

Carr's association with the British Broadcasting Corporation began after he decided no longer to limit himself to writing novels. In 1938 he worked with J. B. Priestley on a film script for the Korda studios, but he never completed his part of the project. His stories depended so much on the intricate relationship of every plot-detail that he found it difficult to share responsibilities with a coauthor. His longtime editor, Joan Kahn, explained that "he had done the planning and plotting, the weaving of his fabric so skillfully, and so much in his own way, that an outsider's suggestions would probably have pulled threads or even left holes." Moreover, Carr had to contend with the changing ideas of film barons about what they wanted in the script. "Why I still preserve some vestige of my reason remains a mystery," Carr wrote to his friend Clayton Rawson after his film experiences. Carr's judgment that filmmakers are "madder than a crate-load of coots" provided the background of a Sir Henry Merrivale novel, *And So To Murder* (1940).

Meanwhile, at the suggestion of his British agents, Carr submitted a three-part Dr. Fell play, "Who Killed Matthew Corbin?," to the BBC. Val Gielgud, head of the BBC's Drama Department from the late 1920s to the middle 1960s, was perhaps the perfect producer (or director, in American terminology) to work with Carr. Gielgud preferred plays to be between forty minutes and an hour in length, but he did not insist on a predetermined format. More importantly as far as Carr was concerned, he allowed the author to control his own script. He encouraged the scriptwriter to be present at the preliminary reading by the cast, to explain his intentions and, whenever necessary, to revise narration and dialogue. Unlike the situation at film studios, the final script matched the intentions of the playwright.

"Who Killed Matthew Corbin?," broadcast in December 1939 and January 1940, is a fine play. It is not included in this book only because its central clue was also used in the later "The Hangman Won't Wait," recently printed in *The Door to Doom and Other Detections*. Although Gielgud wanted his scriptwriters to be sparing with musical bridges and sound effects, Carr was able to set the mood of "Matthew Corbin" with a background of rain, thunder, and "a flourish of music, strong and harsh." A month or so later, Carr followed with "The Black Minute" (the first play in this book), which with its impossible crime and well-hidden murderer is a good introduction to his radio work.

The Second World War had begun in the final months of 1939, and the BBC geared up to produce propaganda plays (one of them featured Milton Rosmer as Hitler; Rosmer later played Dr. Fell on the radio). After the fall of Poland there was a lull in the fighting—newspapers wrote about "The Phony War"—and Carr took the opportunity to visit his family in the United States. But when Germany invaded much of Western Europe in April and May 1940, and sent planes to bomb Britain, Carr returned to England to support the war as a writer. Val Gielgud noted in his diary: "Met John Dickson Carr for lunch at the Ivy. He has come back from the States—a gallant and quite uncalled-for gesture on his part—to see the war through in a country he is fond of, and I've good hope of fixing him up with something in my department."

Besides continuing to write two detective novels a year, Carr regularly provided scripts for the BBC. A few were mysteries, including a serial set in the early nineteenth century entitled "Speak of the Devil," but most were propaganda plays encouraging the British to avoid the black market, explaining the role of women on gunsights, and outlining the life of Heinrich Himmler ("I am Heinrich Himmler. Let me shake your hand. Wouldn't you like to be ruled by me?"). John Dickson Carr and his wife Clarice suffered directly from German attacks during the Battle of Britain. In September 1940 their London house was demolished by a direct hit while the Carrs were in it. Although they lost most of their furniture, they escaped without a scratch. While Clarice Carr joined her family (and their remaining furniture) in Bristol, Carr stayed at the Savage Club in London. After the back of the club was sliced off by a German bomb, Carr moved to Bristol, but German bombers seemed to dog him:

> A bomb landed across the street, removing from our house windows, doors, and roof. The only reason why more damage was not done was . . . a small shed or pavilion which took the main blast. This contained what was left of our furniture, salvaged from our London house. . . . I can imagine the triumphant German airman hurrying back to Goering and saying, "Ich habe busted der resten den furniture von Carr!" And Goering swelling under his medals and saying, "Gut! Sie wilst der Iron Cross getten! Heil Hitler!"

Such events must have added a fillip to Carr's propaganda writing. In February 1941 Carr wrote, "The thing had become monotonous; and both Clarice and I were growing a little fed-up with living constantly in a series of residences bearing some resemblance to a doll's house with the front off." Carr later gained a measure of revenge by writing a propaganda play in which Hitler disappears from a locked room.

The BBC asked Carr to join its staff, but when the United States entered the war after Pearl Harbor, Carr returned to sign up for military service. While waiting for the government to decide how best to use his talents, he agreed to write plays for the Columbia Broadcasting System's *Suspense*—a program that had begun on June 17, 1942, with an adaptation of Carr's novel *The Burning Court*. Carr's own scripts started on October 27 with "Lord of the Witch Doctors," followed a week later with "The Devil in the Summer-House," both of which had earlier been heard on the BBC. His next twenty scripts were written directly for *Suspense* (six of them were recently printed in *The Door to Doom*).

Working for CBS was quite different from Carr's experiences at the BBC. American radio emphasized split-second timing aimed at fitting precisely a thirty-minute or hour format. Rather than downplaying sound effects, *Suspense* emphasized them. Music was used lavishly—*Suspense* had a small orchestra—and knife-chords aroused the listeners' emotions at strategic moments. Each episode opened with the hollow clanging of church bells, fading into the introduction by the bass-voiced narrator, "The Man in Black." Several of Carr's plays ("Cabin B-13," "The Pit and the Pendulum," and "Mr. Markham, Antique

Dealer") became standbys for much of *Suspense*'s twenty-year run. "Cabin B-13," moreover, was adapted as the 1953 Twentieth Century-Fox film *Dangerous Crossing*. Carr's scripts were printed in two anthologies and in early issues of *Ellery Queen's Mystery Magazine*.

Carr, however, found some of CBS's requirements irksome. Above all he objected to the network's fear of offending certain ethnic groups. CBS allowed him to choose criminals who were British, American, or—a safe group to hate in the early 1940s—German; but when Carr had an Italian villain, CBS decided that some of *Suspense*'s listeners would be offended, and he had to rewrite the play. Consequently, Carr may have been relieved when the American government decided how he could best help in the war. In an ironic twist, the authorities who had called him home decided toward the middle of 1943 to send him back to London to continue his propaganda work for the BBC.

Gielgud welcomed his return by producing on August 28, 1943, a version of Carr's *Suspense* play "The Dead Sleep Lightly." The American script, in half an hour, had excellent plot and atmosphere, but it was rather flaccid in its conclusion. For British audiences, Carr lengthened the play to forty minutes, and strengthened it by including Dr. Fell, whose character contrasts with the coldness of the victim; and he ended it with a typical Carrian emphasis on justice rather than the letter of the law.

Carr had already persuaded Gielgud that more of his *Suspense* scripts might be made into a series for the BBC. Gielgud recalled:

> He suggested to me that there might be a place in English programmes for a series of thrillers handled in the American manner, with all the trimmings of atmospheric bass-voiced narrator, knife-chords and other specially composed musical effects, and a regular length of half an hour timed to the split second. My slight experience of American methods made the temptation to compete "on the home ground" irresistible.

As Carr wrote to his American correspondents, the BBC series, *Appointment with Fear,* was simply *Suspense* under a new title. Valentine Dyall became the British "Man in Black," and the series opened on September 11, 1943, with "Cabin B-13." Both Carr and the BBC looked upon *Appointment with Fear* as contributing to the war effort by presenting cozier horrors than Hitler was providing. "These plays," Carr wrote, "are frankly forms of escapism. The present war is seldom or never mentioned; the action takes place against a peacetime security. That, we felt, is the only atmosphere in which a listener can bother about being scared by shadows." Although Carr did not direct the plays himself, his experience with American radio meant that he often helped with sound effects. The second play was his version of Poe's "The Pit and the Pendulum," for which the major problem was creating a realistic *whush* as the pendulum descends toward its victim. After trying in vain to get the proper sound by swinging a golf club in front of the microphone, the sound man finally had to settle for an air hose.

Gielgud was at first worried about how the British public would react to "the unabashed histrionicism" of the plays: "We were told that we would scarify the children. We were rebuked for treating horror with levity." But it turned out that both children and adults loved the shows. The title of the series became familiar enough that at least three British newspapers used it in political cartoons, and jokes using the title received a ready response in the theaters. Valentine Dyall's role as the narrator was so well known that in 1950 he starred in a film entitled *The Man in Black,* which was based on *Appointment with Fear,* though not on a Carr story.

Carr's *Suspense* scripts were soon exhausted, and he wrote a second and then a third series of new plays for *Appointment with Fear.* Meanwhile, he continued preparing propaganda scripts. *The Silent Battle,* a series of six plays broadcast in 1944, deserves to be well remembered. As well as emphasizing the nastiness of the Nazis, *The Silent Battle* focuses on the actions and emotions of the underground front in the occupied countries. All six plays are well plotted, but one is especially noteworthy for Carr's use of his favorite device, the miracle problem. Where would the Polish underground hide a radio so that the most thorough search by the Gestapo would fail to find it? The answer is typically John Dickson Carr: the radio is hidden in the false hunchback of a hurdy-gurdy man.

Carr enjoyed writing for the radio. He had no difficulty inventing plots, and he looked on his scripts as a welcome relaxation from writing novels. Nonetheless, he resigned from the BBC when the war ended in 1945. Spending a day at an office was not the way he liked to work, and he needed the time to begin research for his definitive biography of Sir Arthur Conan Doyle. Moreover, the victory of the Labour Party in the 1945 elections made him dissatisfied with living in England. He equated socialism with herd existence, and no longer did he feel that the values he treasured could be found in postwar Britain. Some of his friends have suggested that he would have been happiest in the eighteenth century, but (as that was impossible) he did the next best thing. He wrote historical detective stories, some of which have a twentieth-century hero transported to the past.

Carr returned to the United States in 1948, and almost immediately he became again associated with the radio. CBS asked him to write plays for a new program called *Cabin B-13* after Carr's popular *Suspense* play. The new series debuted on July 5, 1948, as an eight-week summer replacement, and it was revived for a second group of plays from October 3, 1948, through January 2, 1949. Unfortunately, not much is known about *Cabin B-13*. Sound recordings of only three broadcasts have so far been discovered, and we have the scripts only of those shows that were also used on *Suspense* or *Appointment with Fear*. We wish that we could publish the scripts of "The Dancer from Stamboul," "Nine Black Reasons," "The Street of the Seven Daggers," "Island of Coffins," and "Power of Darkness," but until they show up in some archive, we have to be satisfied—or frustrated—with their intriguing titles.

About the same time, Carr became narrator of the Mutual series *Murder by Experts*, but after he left that show he was no longer involved with American broadcasting. Television was coming to dominate the American media, and Carr refused to write for video broadcasts; perhaps he recalled his unhappy experiences with film scripts. Both British and American television produced adaptations of Carr's stories—most notably a series starring Boris Karloff based on Carr's book *The Department of Queer Complaints*—but he was only indirectly involved in such projects.

Carr's final radio work was for the BBC, which retained (and still retains) dramatic radio. He had returned to England with the election of a Conservative government, and in 1955 he wrote six plays for a revival of *Appointment with Fear*. The BBC went all out to recreate the great wartime program, bringing Valentine Dyall back as The Man in Black, and including the knife-chords and other atmospheric trimmings of the earlier program. Carr wrote some of his best plays for what turned out to be a farewell series. Especially noteworthy is "The Villa of the Damned" in its reversal of a famous impossible-crime gambit. Robert Adey, the bibliographer of locked rooms and other miracle crimes, points out that the problem of a disappearing house has attracted the ingenuity of several authors. In his play, however, Carr does not make the house disappear, only all of its surroundings.

In a book addressed to aspiring radio dramatists, Val Gielgud argued that radio may be the most demanding medium. It takes what Frederic Dannay (who with his cousin Manfred Lee wrote the notable *Ellery Queen* radio shows) called "different muscles" from those used for prose fiction. Writing for the radio, moreover, is far different from preparing scripts for theater, film, and television. A dramatist for the stage can show his audience the setting, the actions of the characters, and the physical clues. The radio playwright, on the other hand, has to suggest everything through sound. He has to be a master of dialogue, of the precise image created by words. Though radio may seem one-dimensional, the scriptwriter has to be in some ways more sophisticated, more in control of his medium, than the author who can appeal to several senses. When a radio play is successful, it is less limited than other forms of drama; it can range as far as the imagination of the listener.

Carr not only knew how far his audience's imagination could range; he counted on it. Some of the plays in this book depend on the listener fooling himself through his own imagination. As with his novels and short stories, Carr planned every element of his radio scripts to produce a precise effect; and thus he expected much from the actors to put the play over. His stage directions and descriptions of characters are specific, and he fretted when an actor did not interpret a character exactly as he had intended. We can sympathize, however, with the actor told by Carr to have a "fat" voice, or the one directed to sound querulous but nonetheless to deserve our respect.

Carr planned exactly how sound effects would influence the mood and define the characters. Often in the plays in this book, Carr introduces a single background sound to lead, or mislead, his audience: the musical glasses in "The Devil's Saint" and the whirl of the roulette wheel in "Death Has Four Faces."

Nine plays from the more than seventy-five of Carr's surviving scripts have been chosen to represent his radio work. The versions are those broadcast in Britain and preserved in the BBC's extensive Play Library, for whose assistance and generosity we are very grateful. The plays are as Carr wrote them, but we have had to make some editorial decisions. Many of the typescripts have handwritten alterations that were accepted and, probably in most cases, suggested by Carr; we have adopted the wording that reads most effectively. Occasionally, too, we have had to make some changes when Carr's descriptions of characters give away too much of the surprise ending, and when stage directions repeat some of the dialogue. Otherwise, we have printed the scripts exactly as broadcast, even including indications of knife-chords and other effects.

Carr's plays are exercises in fair-play ingenuity. Most of the shows, Carr explained, "aim at presenting the evidence fairly and upsetting the applecart with a twist at the end. And all of them deal with diablerie in one form or another." In short, this book brings together the Golden Age of detection and the Golden Age of radio. Nowhere were they better combined than in the plays of John Dickson Carr.

Douglas G. Greene

PREFACE TO
The Black Minute

A séance held in the dark is an ideal setting for a radio mystery, especially one that suggests the supernatural. The audience, like the characters themselves, can hear but not see what is happening. To create
the mood, the announcer asked listeners to turn out their lights as the
play began. Although we cannot ask readers to do the same, it is only
fair to give warning that one of Dr. Fell's main clues involves darkness.

The Black Minute

THE CHARACTERS:

Dr. Gideon Fell	The detective
Sir Francis Church	An elderly scientist
Margery Grey	His niece
Mr. Riven	Student of psychical research
Anna	His housekeeper
Harry Brewster	In the rubber tire business
Taxi driver	

Setting: London, 1940.

(*The sound of a high wind, thin and shrill, continues throughout the following conversation. A taxi approaches and stops.*)

TAXI DRIVER (*hoarse and confidential*): This the 'ouse, miss? Can't see any numbers in this blackout.

MARGERY GREY: Yes, this is the house. I think. (*The voice is that of a girl in her middle twenties: very pleasant, and palpably worried.*)

(*A car door opens and slams. The wind blows shrilly.*)

MARGERY: Here you are.

TAXI DRIVER (*gratefully*): Thank *you*, miss. Like me to 'old a light on the steps while you go up?

MARGERY (*shivering*): No, thanks. I can manage. Good night.

TAXI DRIVER: Good night, miss.

(*The gears grind and the car drives away. Footsteps rasp on stone steps. Then—dull and hollow, giving the impression of depths in the house—the thud of an iron knocker.*)

MARGERY (*to herself, determined but nervous*): So this is the ogre's den! This is—

(*Front door opens. ANNA, the housekeeper, speaks. She has*

a middle-aged, hard, thick, expressionless voice; the voice of a woman who sees much and says little.)

ANNA (*coldly*): Yes?

MARGERY: I want to see Mr. Riven, please.

ANNA: I'm sorry, miss. Mr. Riven isn't at home.

MARGERY (*afraid but insistent*): My name is Margery Grey. I'm Sir Francis Church's niece. We're all coming here for the séance tonight. I'm just a bit early, that's all; and I've got to see Mr. Riven.

ANNA (*enlightened*): Oh. You'd better come in, then.

MARGERY: Thank you. (*Crying out, startled*) Oh!

ANNA: Be careful, miss. Don't stumble. We've got no lights in the house for a minute or two. The fuses blew. Here, take my hand. (*Slight pause; then sardonically*) What's the matter? Not afraid, are you?

MARGERY: Why should I be afraid?

ANNA (*grimly*): That's right, miss. We'll just lock up. . . .
(*The door closes, and a heavy bar is shot into place. This shuts out the noise of the wind, though it can still be heard blowing faintly from time to time.*)

ANNA: Now over here to the stairs. You can feel the stair carpet with your foot. Now up . . . up . . . straight on up . . .
(*Faintly at first, far away and growing a bit louder, but never very loud, we hear the music of a violin playing "Humoresque."*)

MARGERY (*quickly*): What's that?

ANNA (*noncommittally*): It's him. . . . You see that door? Where there's firelight? Go in there and wait. I'll tell him you're here.
(*A door closes, shutting out the sound of the violin.*)

MARGERY (*to herself, bitterly*): Wouldn't you know it? All the stage trappings. Deep carpet and firelight. Suit of Japanese armour with devil mask. Globe and books . . . Drat him! (*In a lower voice, daringly but with conviction*) Damn him! (*The door opens and closes. RIVEN speaks. He has a slow, heavy, deliberate voice, not without amusement underneath; the voice of one who knows how to use words and is aware of their power.*)

RIVEN: Were you calling down curses on *my* head, Miss Grey?

MARGERY (*startled and incredulous*): Are you Mr. Riven?

RIVEN: I am.

MARGERY (*impulsively*): But you don't . . . I mean, you don't look anything like what I'd expected!

RIVEN (*gravely*): My dear young lady, did you expect me to come in wearing a conical hat and a robe covered with signs of the zodiac? (*Laughs*) I am an ordinary person like yourself. Though far from being beautiful like yourself, if you'll allow me to say so.

MARGERY (*still rather incredulous*): You're the medium?

RIVEN: I am a student of psychical research.

MARGERY (*girding up her courage and flinging out at him*): I'll tell you what you are. You're a fake.

(*In the ensuing pause, the wind is heard blowing thinly. RIVEN's voice is still thoughtful, but it is not pleasant.*)

RIVEN: There is no need to back away, Miss Grey. I won't hurt you. Shall we forget what you just said?

MARGERY (*fiercely*): No, we won't! (*Changing her tone*) Please, Mr. Riven, I didn't mean to offend you. I didn't. But I want you to let my uncle alone.

RIVEN (*slowly*): Sir Francis Church is a very distinguished scientist.

MARGERY: Yes, but he's an old man; an old, old man. And I won't have them laughing at him. That's what they're all doing, and you know it.

RIVEN: Indeed?

MARGERY (*desperately*): It's true, and you know it! I shouldn't mind if you were honest and sincere about it. Maybe there is an afterlife. I don't know. Maybe we can get into communication with the dead. I don't know. But you're not like that. Do you know Sir Barton MacNeile?

RIVEN: I have that honor. He is head of the Psychical Research Society.

MARGERY: Well, *he* says you're a fake. He says no honest spiritualist will have anything to do with you. He says . . . (*She breaks off*) Oh, I know I'm doing this badly! I'm only offending you, and all I wanted to do was to appeal to you. Will you let my uncle alone? It's impossible to live with him any more. And it's an awful thing to say, but sometimes I wish he'd—die. (*Slight pause*) Ever since you told him his wife had died of being poisoned . . .

RIVEN (*authoritatively*): Just one moment, Miss Grey. Please understand that, whatever the entities may say when they speak through my mouth, I know nothing of it. . . . Er—I believe you nursed the late Lady Church before she died?

MARGERY: What do you mean by that?

RIVEN (*surprised*): Nothing. I stated a fact.

MARGERY: I don't know what you mean, and I don't care. All I know is that my uncle can't think of anything but trying to get in touch with her. He even thinks he hears her tapping at the window at night, trying to get in. (*Three sharp, quick raps are heard on a pane of glass.*) What was that?

(*Short pause, with the sound of the wind blowing thinly.*)

RIVEN: I heard nothing.

MARGERY (*in a low, steady voice*): Yes, you did. You're trying to scare me. I want to go.

RIVEN: But, my dear young lady, aren't you going to stay for the séance? Sir Francis will be here in a moment. So will young Mr. Harry Brewster (*complacently*), whom I hope to make our latest convert.

MARGERY (*pouncing*): Yes. And so will Dr. Fell.

RIVEN (*sharply*): Who?

MARGERY (*with underlying triumph*): Dr. Gideon Fell. I thought that would make you jump.

RIVEN: You invited this Dr. Fell to my house?

MARGERY: Yes, I did. He's coming with my uncle. Are you afraid to have him here?

RIVEN: I shall welcome him. Believe me, Miss Grey, you misjudge me. I am much maligned. I have no devils concealed up my sleeve. I cannot whistle the dead out of their graves at my will. Of course, if they choose to come to me, that is another matter. (*Three more sharp, quick raps on a pane of glass*) Give me your hand!

MARGERY: Why?

RIVEN: For the last time, I will not hurt you! Give me your hand!

MARGERY (*crying out*): Uncle! Uncle! *Uncle!*

(*Her voice trails off and is lost in the loud whistling of the wind. Again we hear a motorcar draw up and stop.*)

TAXI DRIVER (*confidently*): This is the 'ouse, gentlemen. I brought a young lady 'ere not fifteen minutes ago.

(SIR FRANCIS CHURCH *speaks. His voice is that of an old man—inclined at times to be fretful and querulous, but still strong and far from being senile. It is also that of a man used to commanding and dominating: probably in his earlier years a Tartar. It remains full of suspicion. But he has dignity; and, if you do not like him, you are bound to give him respect.*)

SIR FRANCIS (*suspiciously*): A young lady, you say? That must be my niece.

TAXI DRIVER: Dunno about that, guv'nor. (*Casually*) Tipped 'andsome, though.

SIR FRANCIS: We'll get out here.

(*Car door opens.*)

TAXI DRIVER (*doubtfully*): Excuse me, sir. But can the other gentleman—the stout gentleman—manage to get out of the cab?

DR. FELL (*thunderously intervening*): Sir, that is an implication I resent. (*Warmly*) To be stuck forever in a taxicab . . . to spend the rest of my life in a taxicab . . . to bore holes for my feet and walk about clad in a taxicab . . . is a prospect to make any man shudder. I *can* get out of here. I WILL get out of here. (*Heavy grunt*)

TAXI DRIVER: Thank you, sir. Good night.

(*As the cab goes off,* SIR FRANCIS *speaks doggedly as though continuing an argument.*)

SIR FRANCIS: So you won't be persuaded to believe in the cause, Dr. Fell?

DR. FELL: Sir, I neither believe nor disbelieve.

SIR FRANCIS: Then you're nothing. (*Bitterly*) Hate the cause; sneer at the cause; fight the cause. But don't be indifferent to the cause. (*Changing his tone*) Oh, I know! I was a sceptic myself. I prided myself on being . . . (*still more bitterly*) . . . the cold man of science. I once wrote, "The term 'afterlife' sounds rather like 'anticlimax,' and must, I imagine, amount to much the same thing."

DR. Fell: And you don't believe that any longer?

SIR FRANCIS (*simply*): I am reborn. Elsie talks to me.

DR. FELL: Elsie?

SIR FRANCIS: My wife. She died four years ago.

DR. FELL (*quietly*): Just a moment, Sir Francis, before you lift that knocker. (*Slight pause*) Frankly, you puzzle me.

SIR FRANCIS: Oh? How?

DR. FELL: I have had some slight acquaintance with you, now, for a good many years. You're a fighter. You are also an intelligent man. It would take a very superior brand of tomfoolery to deceive you. (Sir Francis *snorts, but* Dr. Fell *goes on.*) Before coming here, I obtained some information about this Mr. Riven of yours.

Sir Francis: From Lord Senlac? I had Riven at Senlac House the other night.

Dr. Fell: No. From Scotland Yard.

Sir Francis (*sharply*): Scotland Yard?

Dr. Fell: Yes. Now you know my state of mind. Shall we go in? (*The wind whistles thinly.*)

Sir Francis (*with concentrated bitterness*): That, eh? I see. The police persecute Riven. Even the spiritualists persecute him. And therefore I am to turn away from the pioneer. I'm to get down on my knees like another scientist and deny that the earth moves. Well, I won't do it. I know what I know. I've never been afraid of ridicule in my life, and I'm not afraid of it now. (*This seems to have exhausted him. His voice grows fretful.*) Things are hard sometimes. Very hard on a man. We must have a creed, Fell. Even you must have a creed. What do you affirm?

Dr. Fell: I affirm—

Sir Francis: Yes?

Dr. Fell (*in a sharper, clearer tone*): I affirm that I just heard somebody scream.

(*The whistle of the wind is mingled with the heavy banging of the iron knocker. This fades away into* Margery's *voice.*)

Margery (*frightened but triumphant*): There, you see! That's my uncle downstairs now. I can hear his voice.

Riven (*mildly protesting*): But, my dear young lady, you act as though you thought I were trying to molest you.

Margery: Aren't you?

Riven: Hardly . . . (*significantly*) . . . at this moment. Excuse me. (*A door opens, and* Riven *raises his voice.*) Sir Francis? This way.

(*A soft but heavy bump, as of someone falling on carpeted stairs. An exclamation of pain.* Sir Francis's *voice, angry and querulous, comes closer.*)

Sir Francis: Riven! Where the devil are you, Riven? What do you mean, keeping all the lights out in this house? (*Still more querulously*) Tripped and nearly broke my knee on those stairs of yours. (*In pain*) Ffff! No, I won't shake hands. Got my hand all over dirt. (*Breaking off*) What are you doing here, girl?

MARGERY: You promised I could attend the séance, Uncle Francis.

SIR FRANCIS: Went out without your dinner, didn't you? All right! Sit down there and be quiet. (*Pauses*) Riven, this is Dr. Gideon Fell.

DR. FELL: How do you do?

RIVEN: I am honoured.

MARGERY (*under her breath*): You're a bad-tempered old man, that's what you are. *I* won't try to help you.

SIR FRANCIS (*sharply*): What did you say, Margery?

MARGERY (*submissively*): Nothing, Uncle Francis.

RIVEN: I am sorry about the lights, Sir Francis. The fuses will be mended in a moment. In the meantime, we are waiting for Mr. Harry Brewster.

MARGERY: Listen: There's someone else at the front door now. (*Distantly a heavy door is heard to open and close.*)

VOICE: Hullo, hullo, hullo! Anybody at home?

MARGERY (*half-laughing*): That's Harry Brewster all right.

(HARRY *talks himself up into the room. He is a brisk, breezy, bouncing young man in his late twenties; likeable but loud, confident, and rather credulous.*)

HARRY: Nice of you to let me in, Anna. Anna, you get older and prettier every day . . . (*Imitating a bus conductor*) Mind the step, madam! (*Bursting in*) Hel-lo, everybody! Where's the Grand Goblin and Rainmaker?

RIVEN: Good evening, Mr. Brewster.

HARRY (*with breezy heartiness*): Wot-cher, old cock? Hello, Margery. Evening, Sir Francis. Who's this?

RIVEN: Mr. Brewster, Dr. Gideon Fell.

HARRY (*breaking off, impressed*): I say! Is it? Hel-lo, Doctor. Going to catch another murderer for us?

(*Again there are three sharp, vicious raps on the pane of glass.*)

HARRY (*surprised*): Hullo! Something seems to be trying to get in.

SIR FRANCIS (*rasping*): Don't talk like that, you young fool! Do you want to attract evil forces?

HARRY (*hurt*): No offence, Sir Francis; no-o-o offence. Just trying to keep the party merry and bright. (*Amused*) The last time they turned Dr. Fell loose to catch a murderer, he nailed a BBC announcer. When that happens, nobody's safe. (*Confidentially*) What do you think about all this, Doctor? Spooks, I mean. Are you a spook-fancier?

DR. FELL (*amused*): At least, Mr. Brewster, I gather that you are a sceptic?

HARRY: Me? (*With sudden intense solemnity*) No, no, no!

DR. FELL: No?

HARRY: Not a bit of it. What I say is, these things can't be taken too seriously. Now, I'm a modern man. A practical man. (*Breaking off to explain*) I'm in the rubber tire business, Doctor. Here's my card. Dear old Lady Church set me up in business, bless her. (*Returns to his theme*) Well, what I say is, how do we know about these things? I believe in an afterlife. And what's believing in an afterlife *but* believing in ghosts, if you see what I mean? Or, if it's not ghosts, it's something. Maybe a scientific force. Maybe we'll discover it. No, indeed. (*Proudly*) I'm a practical man; I can believe anything.

RIVEN (*drily*): Very aptly put. Then shall we proceed to the test?

SIR FRANCIS (*vacantly*): Yes. I feel that there will be visitors tonight.

RIVEN: First, let us see if the lights work. (*A sharp click*) Yes, they're on now. And I have a word to say in all humility to all of you. (*But he does not sound humble.*) I have been accused of being a fraud and a charlatan. (*Arrogantly, as there is a slight murmur of protest*) Oh, yes, I have! That charge has not been made against me in any of the great houses into which Sir Francis has introduced me. But it has been made here. (*Hypnotically*) Now please understand one thing. When I am in my trance, I know nothing of what goes on. If you waked me, you might kill me. I therefore propose to answer the scoffers in their own language. I propose to submit to a test in which any fraud would be impossible. You see that door over there?

DR. FELL: We see it.

RIVEN: That door leads to a small room, without windows. It has plaster walls and a bare board-floor. In the way of furniture, it contains only some chairs, a table, and a gramophone.

SIR FRANCIS: *She* will be there.

RIVEN: We shall bolt the door on the inside. I shall ask to be tied with cords to one of the chairs. We will take one further precaution which will make it absolutely impossible for me to move. Are you ready?

(*The following three voices speak swiftly on the heels of each other.*)

SIR FRANCIS: *I* am ready, by heaven.

HARRY (*through his teeth*): Carry on, old son.

MARGERY: No! . . . Yes! All right.

(*A door opens.*)

RIVEN (*with smiling courtesy*): Then—will you walk into my parlour?

(*The sound of the wind rises and falls strongly.*)

MARGERY: It's awfully cold in here.

RIVEN: Are you now convinced, Mr. Brewster, that I am tied to this chair in such a way that I cannot possibly move?

HARRY: Ho! *Am* I! (*In an aside*) Margery, if he can get out of that, he's a ghost himself. I've even got his fingers tied together with thread.

RIVEN: If you please! We will take one further precaution. Miss Grey, will you reach into the upper right-hand pocket of my waistcoat? Don't be afraid. You will find there a small bottle of luminous paint. Have you got it?

MARGERY: Yes.

RIVEN: Please take the brush and make a plain mark in luminous paint on each side of my collar—just beside the necktie. I must apologize for these absurdities, gentlemen. But I want you to be sure. Even if I could dislodge any of these cords, I could scarcely move without being seen. You agree? (*Three voices almost simultaneously say "yes." DR. FELL does not speak.*) Good! Then will the four of you sit down round the table? My chair will be a little way back from you all. (*Scraping of chairs on a bare board-floor.*) One moment! Mr. Brewster, will you go and start the gramophone? It will stop itself. When you hear my command, turn out the lights and come back to the group round the table.

MARGERY: Do you want us to clasp hands?

RIVEN: That will not be necessary.

SIR FRANCIS: I think it will be. Listen to me. (*With the ring of authority*) I've sat quietly by. I've heard you called a charlatan and myself an old fool. There are forces tonight, and

they're bad. I want a chain of linked hands round this table.
Margery, give me your hand.

MARGERY: You got your hand awfully dirty on those stairs, Uncle
Francis.

SIR FRANCIS: Never mind that. Give me your hand. Now you,
Fell, on my other side. Harry, attend to those lights and
complete the circle. Quickly!

(*Faintly at some distance away, three more raps are followed by the noise of glass shattering.*)

HARRY: It seems to have got in.

RIVEN (*rather drowsily*): That was the other room. There are no
windows here. Start the gramophone, Mr. Brewster. (*A
sound of footsteps on the bare board-floor. Then the scratch
of a gramophone needle as the disk starts to turn, but it does
not yet play.*)

RIVEN: Now. Turn . . . out . . . the . . . lights . . . please.

(*More footsteps and a click. The footsteps return to the
table.*)

HARRY: Your hand, Margery. Your other hand, Dr. Fell. I felt—

SIR FRANCIS (*dully*): Be quiet. Be quiet.

(*After a pause, the music swells out, but not at all loudly.*)

RIVEN (*drowsily*): I shall be leaving you soon. Do not attempt to
speak to me afterwards.

(*The music still plays for some seconds.*)

MARGERY (*in a whisper*): I felt something.

SIR FRANCIS (*fiercely*): Sh-h!

MARGERY: Those luminous-paint spots. They look like eyes. I
can't stand—

RIVEN (*still more drowsily*): Do not attempt to speak to me
after—

(*The speech ends in a kind of bubbling screech, rising to a
cry of agony, but choked thickly as though by liquid in
mouth and throat.*)

HARRY (*breathing*): For God's sake, what was it?

DR. FELL: I think we had better have the lights on.

SIR FRANCIS: Don't break the circle! Don't break—

DR. FELL (*grimly*): At the same time, I think we had better have
the lights on. Mr. Riven!

(*No reply.*)

HARRY (*struck with superstitious terror in spite of himself*): I
say, sir, shall I—?

DR. FELL: Yes.

(*Scraping of chairs and blundering footsteps. A chair is knocked over.*)

DR. FELL: Hurry!

HARRY: Got it!

(*A switch clicks sharply. Silence except for the music. Then* MARGERY *screams. The gramophone slows down, scratching hollowly, and stops.*)

HARRY (*after a pause; and in a low incredulous voice; almost guilty*): I don't. . . believe it.

MARGERY (*not loudly; too tense to be hysterical*): That . . . isn't blood, is it? All over Mr. Riven's neck?

SIR FRANCIS: He's holding his head in an uncommonly queer way.

DR. FELL: That, my friend, is not part of his head. That's the handle of the knife. He's been stabbed through the throat.

MARGERY: He's falling sideways.

DR. FELL: He can't fall. Not held up by all those cords.

HARRY (*with heavy and hollow incredulity*): I don't believe it. He's playing a joke on us. (*Tentatively*) And a poor joke too. Rotten bad form, if you ask me. (*Insistently*) Come on, old chap! Say something.

MARGERY: Don't touch him!

HARRY: But it can't be. You mean somebody came in here, and . . . ?

DR. FELL: The door is bolted on the inside.

(*Quick footsteps on the floor. Noise of a bolt being shot back, and into its socket again.*)

HARRY: It's true. (*Blustering scepticism is fighting with superstitious terror.*) Go on! It's a joke. I still don't believe it. I'm not going to let you say that one of us . . .

MARGERY: Harry, that can't be. (*Slowly reflecting*) I had Uncle Francis's hand in my left hand, and Harry's hand in my right. I was holding tight.

DR. FELL: That, Miss Grey, is quite true. I can testify that I had Sir Francis's hand on my right and Mr. Brewster's hand on my left.

HARRY (*startled*): And I had you on my right and Margery on my left. Neither of you let go.

SIR FRANCIS (*very tired*): If it's any satisfaction to your (*bitterly*) practical minds, I can tell you that the circle was complete. I held my niece's hand at the right and Dr. Fell's at the left. We formed a closed chain.

HARRY: But—

DR. FELL (*sternly and heavily, quieting possible panic*): One moment. (*Murmurs subside*) We shall all have questions to answer shortly. Let's be quite clear about one thing from the start . . . Did anyone let go another hand at any time? Even for a second?

HARRY: No, definitely not!

MARGERY: Never!

SIR FRANCIS: Not for a tenth of a second.

HARRY (*stupidly*): Then there's nothing for it. He didn't stab himself; not trussed up like that. And where did the knife come from? Someone must have sneaked in—

DR. FELL: Need I remind you, sir, that the door is bolted on the inside?

(*Pause.*)

SIR FRANCIS: My dear friends. My good foolish friends. (*Wearily*) Do you need to be told who killed him? Fell, come here and look at this knife.

DR. FELL: Be careful. I advise you not to touch him either.

SIR FRANCIS: What does it matter? A little dirt. A little blood. A little span of life composed of the two . . . Here's a man you thought was a charlatan. He's dead.

HARRY: Well, you needn't look at me like that. I didn't kill him.

MARGERY: Then who did?

HARRY: I don't know. But I mean to find out. I'm a practical man, and I'm not going to be put upon. (*Almost pleading, as though urging someone to give up a tedious joke*) Come on, now? Who let go somebody's hand? Did you, Margery?

MARGERY: No, I tell you.

HARRY: Dr. Fell?

DR. FELL (*sternly*): For the second time, young man, no. Besides you don't seem to see the difficulties in the way of that. If one of us did such a thing, he would require two accomplices—one on each side of him. I'm afraid it won't do.

HARRY: But the thing's impossible.

SIR FRANCIS: By ordinary standards, yes.

HARRY: Ordinary standards?

SIR FRANCIS: Yes. And if you want to see how impossible . . .

what *you* call impossible . . . come closer and look at the knife. (*Fiercely*) Oh, come, man! Will you let an old fool look where you daren't? . . . That's right. . . . The handle of that knife is made of polished steel, as bright as new silver. If you don't mind getting close to him, bend down and breathe on the handle. Yes, I said breathe on it! . . . You see?

HARRY: What about it?

SIR FRANCIS: There are no fingerprints on the handle.

HARRY (*after confused thought*): But look here! Gloves . . . or a handkerchief . . .

SIR FRANCIS: A handkerchief, or even gloves, would have left smudges. There are no smudges. (*Vacantly*) No human hand held that knife.

HARRY: You're not trying to tell us he was murdered by a . . .
(*A sharp, heavy knocking at the door interrupts him.*)

MARGERY (*now near hysteria*): Is it coming for the rest of us?

HARRY (*in a commonsense voice*): Nonsense, old girl. It's only Anna. The housekeeper or maid or whatever she is.

MARGERY: Then why don't you open the door?

HARRY: I will. I—
(*The knocking begins again. We hear hesitant footsteps, the sound of a bolt shot back, and the door sharply opened.*)

HARRY (*with a quick breath, as though he half expected someone else*): It's Anna. (*Angrily*) What did I tell you?

ANNA: Excuse me, sir. I heard a kind of sound I shouldn't have heard. Is anything . . .
(*She breaks off, evidently catching sight of RIVEN. The exclamation she gives is not loud, nor anything like a scream; it is more like that of someone being hurt, but it is very definite.*)

DR. FELL: Yes. Someone has killed Mr. Riven. You had better go for the police.

ANNA: I'll dial 999. I've always wanted to dial 999.

DR. FELL: You don't seem very surprised.

ANNA: Me? Naow. I'm not surprised. (*Thoughtfully, without pity*) Through the throat, eh? He always was one for talking. (*The door closes.*)

SIR FRANCIS: I must get out of here.

DR. FELL: Steady, my lad. Take it easy.

SIR FRANCIS (*brusquely*): I'm quite all right. Just a bit queasy, that's all. (*Shivers a little*) I want to get out of this room! It must be deadly cold in here, even for you young people. Can't we at least go into Riven's study?

DR. FELL: Why not? But I don't think any of us had better go further than the study.

SIR FRANCIS (*snapping at him*): Still materialistic, eh?

DR. FELL: I don't think you quite understand my attitude towards these matters. I am very sympathetic towards supernatural happenings . . . when they are genuine supernatural happenings.

HARRY: When they are—

DR. FELL: Let me make it clearer. Suppose you tell me that the ghost of Julius Caesar appeared to Brutus before the Battle of Philippi and warned him of approaching death. All I can say is that I know nothing about it. But suppose you tell me that the ghost of Julius Caesar walked into the cutlery department at Selfridge's, bought a stainless-steel knife, paid for it with spectral banknotes, and then stabbed Brutus in the middle of Oxford Street. All I shall beg leave to murmur, gently, is: rubbish. You cannot mix the two worlds like that. (*More sternly*) This was a human crime, planned by a human being. Don't you see that those two luminous points on Riven's collar showed the murderer . . . or murderess . . . exactly where to strike?

MARGERY (*in a low voice*): In the dark?

DR. FELL: In the dark.

HARRY: But, hang it, Riven himself suggested using the luminous paint!

DR. FELL: Yes. After careful prompting by somebody before we arrived. How else did he happen to have that bottle so conveniently in his pocket?

HARRY: Prompted by . . . ?

DR. FELL: The murderer.

MARGERY: But, Dr. Fell, there was nobody here before the rest of you arrived. (*Laughs*) Except me, of course.

SIR FRANCIS (*curtly*): Be good enough, Margery, not to speak until you're spoken to. . . . Are you telling us, my friend, that you know how this crime was managed?

DR. FELL: I rather think so.

SIR FRANCIS: Are you saying that somebody got in through that bolted door after all?

DR. FELL: No.

SIR FRANCIS (*with increasing shrillness*): Do you mean that one of us got a hand loose in order to stab Riven?

DR. FELL: No.

(*The wind is heard thinly.*)

HARRY (*not loudly*): In just about one minute, I'm going to give a yell and go mad. If you don't want to see me rolling on the hearth rug, say what you mean. . . . I suppose it wasn't suicide?

DR. FELL: No. (*Sincerely*) Believe me, I am not making mysteries. You have made the mysteries. Your minds work like the minds of . . . shall we say? . . . modern dictators. The old-time dictator first started wars and then won medals. The modern dictator first puts on medals and then starts wars. That is your trouble. You have got the crime turned the wrong way round.

MARGERY (*helplessly*): No, Harry, don't look at me. *I* don't know what he's talking about. When we heard Riven utter that horrible cry . . .

DR. FELL (*abruptly*): One moment. How do you know it was Riven who uttered the cry?

HARRY: *What?*

DR. FELL (*in a louder, slower voice*): I said, what reason have you for supposing that it was Riven who uttered the cry? (*Pause.*)

HARRY (*dazed*): But . . . wasn't it?

DR. FELL: You see, that was what the murderer wanted you to think. You heard a terrible kind of screech, which seemed to have death in it. Presently we turned on the lights and found a man with a knife in his neck. So we assumed what was not true. The murderer knew that the source of sound cannot be located in the dark. It was the murderer who let out that appalling cry. Riven, who was supposed to be in a trance, could not speak and ask what had happened. And we . . . including that poor, blind fool, myself . . . we fell straight into the trap. We broke up the circle. It was at least eight seconds before the lights could be turned on. And during that interval, the murderer merely leaned across and stabbed Riven through the neck. The luminous marks on the collar showed him exactly where to strike.

HARRY (*hollowly*): I don't believe that. You can't prove it. (*Breaking off*) *Who* did that?

DR. FELL: Before I answer that question . . .

SIR FRANCIS (*very coolly*): Yes?

DR. FELL: Before I answer that question, I should like to look at Margery's hand.

MARGERY: No, you don't. Why do you want to look at it? That's the second time tonight somebody's asked. Riven wanted to. Why? There's nothing on them—either of them. Look! They're perfectly clean.

DR. FELL (*heavily*): They are . . . Mr. Brewster, you tell me that you are in the rubber tire business. I think I have your card here. Then you would know something about liquid rubber?

HARRY (*harshly*): Yes, I do. What about it?

MARGERY (*reflecting*): Harry, he was sitting just behind *you*.

DR. FELL (*sharply*): One moment. Now, Mr. Brewster, suppose a murderer, after the fashion of many continental criminals, were to paint his fingers and a part of his hand with liquid rubber? He would leave no fingerprints, I think. Not even fabric-mark traces. It would form a thin coating, not even discernible to the touch. The one thing the murderer could not disguise would be its color. What is the color of liquid rubber?

HARRY (*blankly*): Why it's . . . smudgy kind of stuff. Medium or dark grey in color, rather like . . . (*As the meaning of this flashes over him, he hesitates and then brings out the word with a jerk of inspiration.*) . . . *dirt!*

MARGERY (*crying out*): No!

DR. FELL: Exactly. Then the murderer is the man who staged that unnecessary fall on the stairs, to account for the large amount of "dirt" on his right hand. He is the man who . . . though he was tightly holding Miss Grey's hand for some time during the séance . . . transferred no trace of that "dirt" to her left hand. See for yourself. He is the man who refused to wash his hands before the crime, but wanted to get out of the room afterwards. To wash his hands! He is the man who has that betraying stuff on his fingers now. (*Wearily, without triumph*) In short, Sir Francis Church.

(*Below and distantly, the iron knocker on the front door begins to pound.*)

MARGERY: Uncle Francis! Look at me! Look round!

SIR FRANCIS (*calmly*): Yes, my dear?

MARGERY: Aren't you going to say anything? Don't just sit there and nod at the fire. Aren't you going to tell him it's not true?

SIR FRANCIS: Why, my dear, what he says *is* true.

MARGERY: I don't believe it.

SIR FRANCIS (*with a cynicism so deep that it sounds almost careless*): A little dirt. A little blood. A little span of life composed of the two. I've nothing much to lose there. But for a man to be forced to lose the one thing in life he knows to be of any value, his intellectual self-respect . . . (*Breaking off*) Margery, you're over twenty-one. It's time you faced at least some of the facts. (*Bluntly*) I killed my wife. And that swine in there knew it.

MARGERY (*wildly*): Don't say anything more! Keep your voice down. I can hear Anna coming now. She's . . .

ANNA (*interrupting, with subdued triumph*): That's the police at the door. They said they were sending the inspector from the divisional station. Shall I bring 'em up?

(*The door knocker pounds again.*)

SIR FRANCIS (*almost affably*): Bring them up, Anna. Bring them up! This is quite a triumph for you, Dr. Fell.

DR. FELL: No. Believe me; I don't want triumphs like this. (*Bitterly*) So it was blackmail, then? That's what they said about him at Scotland Yard.

SIR FRANCIS (*almost surprised*): Blackmail? (*Contemptuously*) If it had been the ordinary kind of blackmail, do you think I should have minded? Oh, no. I should have paid. But do you know what that man wanted? He wanted to be known as a great medium. He wanted the world to think he had made a convert of me. He wanted me to introduce him into the houses of my friends as a great medium. (*With rising intensity*) He wanted a man of science to babble the degrading nonsense he put into my mouth. He even compelled *me* . . . the one person whose honesty everyone trusted; yes, trusted . . . to play his paltry little parlour tricks while he sat tied in a chair. If you can think of any way for Frank Church to sink lower than that, just tell me what it is.

MARGERY (*murmuring*): Then that was why . . .

SIR FRANCIS: That was why. It surprised him very much when I insisted on our linking hands round the table tonight. But he learned the reason presently. (*Reflectively*) I don't mind what they do now. Even when I stand in a dock . . .

DR. FELL: Need you stand in a dock?

SIR FRANCIS: What do you mean by that?

DR. FELL: If you killed your wife, you deserve to be hanged. But you don't deserve this. You have been a great man, and I will not see you shamed.

(*The loud banging at the front door begins again.* ANNA's *voice is heard distantly, calling angrily.*)

ANNA: All right, not so fast! I'm coming.

DR. FELL: There is still time if you hurry. Get out of here quickly. Scrub that stuff off your hands. Then come back here and tell what story you like. I am no policeman. Let them find out who killed Riven if they can.

SIR FRANCIS (*incredulously*): You . . . mean . . . that?

MARGERY (*frantically*): Of course he means it! So do all of us. Only hurry, hurry, hurry! They're . . .

(*The bar is drawn back on the big door below, and we hear it creak open.*)

ANNA (*distantly*): You'd better come in, the lot of you. Straight upstairs.

SIR FRANCIS (*with growing incredulity*): Do you support this too, Harry?

(*No reply.* SIR FRANCIS's *voice grows harsh.*)

SIR FRANCIS: Well, what is it? Do you support this or don't you?

HARRY: I don't like it, sir, and that's flat. But, if Margery says so, I'll stand by you. (*Hastily*) Only for Lord's sake clear out of here quickly, before they catch you with that stuff on your hands.

MARGERY: Sh-h! Hurry!

SIR FRANCIS (*with maddening deliberation*): What about Anna?

DR. FELL: The good Anna is undoubtedly an old accomplice of Riven's. Also, it was undoubtedly Anna who made all those very crude and clumsy rappings on the window—with the aid of another window, an air-well, and a broomstick. Let her take her broomstick and fly away on it.

MARGERY (*screaming*): They're nearly at the door.

SIR FRANCIS (*calmly*): You're wrong, my dear. They're in the room. . . . (*Breaking off*) Good evening, gentlemen. Come in. (*Blandly*) Whichever of you is the inspector, I wish to give myself up for murder. The question is, will you be able

to prove it in court? I have just one small request to make
before we go. Do you mind if I wash a pair of exceedingly
dirty hands?

(*We hear no reply, but* SIR FRANCIS's *voice takes on a curious
inflection which we do not quite interpret, and are not intended to interpret.*)

SIR FRANCIS: You don't mind? Thank you. Thank you *so* much.

February 13, 1940.

Can a room kill? Wilkie Collins first posed this question in his classic story "A Terribly Strange Bed," but John Dickson Carr probably rang the most changes on it. He wrote two novels, a short story, and two radio-plays, each solving the problem of the murderous room in a different way. When "The Devil's Saint" was broadcast in the United States, Peter Lorre was perfectly cast as the sinister Count Kohary, and everyone who heard that version will probably recall the soft menace of his voice against the gaiety of a fancy-dress ball.

If the devil does have saints, whom does he choose?

The Devil's Saint

THE CHARACTERS:

Lord Edward Whiteford	Son of the Earl of Cray
Stephen Kohary	Hungarian Count
Ileana	His niece
Madame Fley	His housekeeper
Dr. Saulomon	A physician
Driver	

Setting: Paris and Touraine, 1927.

NARRATOR: Paris, fifteen years ago. (*Music up and down*) Paris as it used to be. When lights twinkled from the old Trocadero to the hill of Sacre Coeur. When taxicabs honked, and the beat of tangos swayed, and Chinese lanterns gleamed above the lake in the Bois. When, in short, you and I were young. (*Slight pause*) Come then to the President's Ball at the Opera. St. Catherine's Day, 1927. A fancy-dress ball at the Opera, filling these marble halls with a multitude of masks and a multitude of dreams. The mosaic decorations are no less bright than the colours that weave here, Harlequin and Columbine, Cleopatra and the Musketeers. In the great marble foyer—remember it?—they have set out little tables and lines of palms behind which you may sit screened. Look at one such table. A young man, wearing the scarlet-and-gold uniform of an English Guard's officer in Wellington's day. A dark-haired young girl, in the costume of a Bacchante. And, as we approach . . .

(*Faint murmur in the background, gradually fading out through the following.*)

ILEANA (*not very convincingly*): Ned, don't! Please! You mustn't.

WHITEFORD: Why not? You don't really mind, do you?

ILEANA: No, of course I don't mind. Only you mustn't.

WHITEFORD (*quietly*): Look here, Ileana. We've got to settle this thing. You *have* enjoyed being here tonight, haven't you?

ILEANA: I've loved it! After being cooped up at my uncle's place in the country, it's like heaven!

WHITEFORD: All right! When I take you back to the hotel, I'm going to face this dragon uncle of yours tonight.

ILEANA: No! No! You mustn't!

WHITEFORD: I'm going to say that you and I intend to get married, and that's that.

ILEANA (*quietly*): I can't marry you, Ned. I've told you that.

WHITEFORD (*desperately*): Yes, but why not? Give me just one good reason.

ILEANA: Because . . . I can't. My uncle wouldn't like it.

WHITEFORD: And that seems to you a good enough reason?

ILEANA: Yes.

WHITEFORD: This uncle of yours . . . what's his name?

ILEANA: Count Stephen Kohary.

WHITEFORD: He's a Hungarian, I think you said?

ILEANA: Yes. So am I. My mother was English.

WHITEFORD: What's he like, actually?

ILEANA (*hesitating*): He's—a little eccentric. Please don't misunderstand. He's a scholar and a wit and a historian. Only—he's a little eccentric. He . . . (*Breaking off*) Ned!

WHITEFORD: What is it?

ILEANA: There he is now!

WHITEFORD: Your uncle?

ILEANA (*agitated*): Yes! The tall man in plain evening clothes, with the Order of the Golden Fleece across his chest.

WHITEFORD: I see him. He looks as black as a thunder-cloud.

ILEANA: He's throwing those two dressed as devils aside as though they didn't exist. . . . Give me my mask. Quick! Before he sees us.

WHITEFORD: No, Ileana.

ILEANA: Why not?

WHITEFORD: We'd better face this out now. Sit still.
    (*Slight pause. Count Stephen Kohary has a heavy, slow-speaking, slightly accented voice.*)

KOHARY (*levelly*): Good evening, Ileana.

ILEANA (*confused*): Good evening, Uncle Stephen. Uncle . . . may I present Ned Whiteford?

WHITEFORD: How do you do, sir?

KOHARY (*flatly*): How do you do? . . . Ileana, do you think that costume is quite the thing to wear in public?

ILEANA (*quickly*): Why not?

KOHARY: An older generation might call it immodest. It looks like . . .

ILEANA: Like what?

KOHARY: Nothing! Will you go and get your cloak?

ILEANA: Uncle, *please* don't make me go home so soon. It's hardly eleven o'clock!

KOHARY (*suavely*): I was not asking you to go home, my dear. I was merely asking you to put on a wrap.

ILEANA: All right. I'll get it. You stay and talk to Ned.

KOHARY (*grimly*): I shall be delighted.

WHITEFORD: Will you sit down, sir?

KOHARY: Thank you. You seem to have had quite a gathering at this table.

WHITEFORD: Yes. Some friends of mine from the embassy. They're upstairs dancing now.

KOHARY (*agreeably*): Glasses, glasses, and still more glasses. I was quite an adept once at musical glasses. Have you ever tried it, young man? You take a spoon, like this, and . . .

(*Several tinkling bell-notes from glass, suggesting scale.*)

WHITEFORD (*awkwardly*): Forgive me, sir. There's something I'd like to ask you.

KOHARY: Yes?

(*More glass notes.*)

WHITEFORD: I don't exactly know how to say this, so I'd better say it in the shortest way. I want to marry your niece.

(*Short, sharp crash of breaking glass.*)

WHITEFORD: Look out, sir! You've smashed one of the glasses!

KOHARY (*repressed*): A few francs will pay for it. There are other things with a higher value.

WHITEFORD (*pleading*): Now just a minute, sir, before you fly off the handle!

KOHARY: Was I about to "fly off the handle"? You surprise me.

WHITEFORD: I'm sorry.

KOHARY (*politely*): Not at all.

WHITEFORD (*embarrassed*): Maybe I ought to mention that my full name is Lord Edward Whiteford. My father is the Earl of Cray.

(*More glass notes.*)

KOHARY: Indeed.

WHITEFORD: I only mention that to show we're—well! Respectable enough. The British ambassador will vouch for me, if you'd like to ring him up.

KOHARY: And perhaps *I* ought to mention: I have always kept Ileana carefully guarded from the world.

WHITEFORD: Almost too carefully guarded, don't you think?

KOHARY: That, young man, depends on my reasons.

WHITEFORD (*despairingly*): Sorry again!

KOHARY: You have known Ileana . . . how long?

WHITEFORD: Four days.

KOHARY (*drily*): Four days! You would not choose a business partner in four days. You would not even buy a motorcar in that time. Yet you want to marry!

WHITEFORD: We know our own minds, sir.

KOHARY: Then you know more than the wisest men of this world. However! As one whose dearest wish is Ileana's happiness . . .

WHITEFORD (*intently*): I hope it is, Count Kohary.

KOHARY (*sharply*): You doubt what I say?

WHITEFORD: No, sir. Go on.

KOHARY: Let me make you a counter-proposition. I own an estate in Touraine, not far from Paris. A chateau, a few hundred acres, fishing, a good stable of horses . . .

WHITEFORD: I know. Ileana told me.

KOHARY: Then here is my suggestion. Why not come down and visit us for a week or two?

WHITEFORD (*surprised*): That's very decent of you, sir.

(*The spoon begins to play a tune on the glasses. This tune, ringing slowly, can be discerned as the slow waltz from "Danse Macabre."*)

KOHARY: Not at all. If at the end of that time you are not cured of this infatuation . . .

WHITEFORD (*fiercely*): It's not an infatuation! I swear it's not!

KOHARY: If at the end of that time you are not cured . . . *permanently* . . . of this feeling, you may take Ileana with my blessing. That's fair, isn't it?

WHITEFORD: It's more than fair. I don't know how to thank you!

KOHARY: Don't try. (*Softly*) There is just one thing, however, I feel bound to mention now.

WHITEFORD: Yes, sir?

KOHARY: At the Chateau d'Azay there is a certain bedroom, high up in the east tower. We call it the Tapestry Room.

WHITEFORD: Well, sir?

KOHARY: Would you have any objection to sleeping in that room?

WHITEFORD (*amused*): Lord, no! Why? Is it haunted or anything like that?

KOHARY: Not exactly haunted. No.

WHITEFORD: Then what's the matter with it?

KOHARY: In the way of comfort, nothing. A Prince of the Church has slept there, and a cabinet minister, and a hanging judge. I merely wished to make sure you were not afflicted with any foolish—superstitions.

WHITEFORD (*as though grinning*): You can count on that, sir. No superstitions at all.

KOHARY: Then in that case, if you don't mind, I shall say good night. I think I can trust you to bring Ileana safely to the hotel.

(*A growing murmur of voices in the background.*)

KOHARY (*sharply*): In the meantime, look there! Look all about us! Crowds of our fellow-guests, pouring down the main staircase. Shapes of nightmare. Shapes of delirium. Great goblin masks where only the eyes move. Mightn't you be terrified if you could look inside those painted masks to the real faces they hide?

WHITEFORD: No, I don't think so. They're only ordinary people like ourselves.

KOHARY (*amused*): That, sir, is where you make your mistake. I shall expect you for the weekend. Good night.

ILEANA (*off, calling softly*): Ned! Ned!

WHITEFORD (*indulgently*): It's all right, Ileana. You can come out from behind the palms.

ILEANA (*on, nervously*): What was he saying? I couldn't hear.

WHITEFORD: Ileana, it couldn't be better. He's a very decent old boy actually. And he's invited me to the Chateau d'Azay.

ILEANA: Did he say anything about . . . the Tapestry Room?

WHITEFORD: Yes. He asked me if I'd mind sleeping there.

ILEANA: And you said?

WHITEFORD (*surprised*): I said I didn't mind. Naturally.

ILEANA (*fiercely*): You mustn't *do* it, Ned! I won't let you do it!

WHITEFORD: Why the devil not?

ILEANA: Because everybody who sleeps in that room . . . dies.

(*Knife-chord, and laughter—hollow laughter—from many persons in the background.*)

WHITEFORD: Are you serious?

ILEANA: Don't I *look* serious? You mustn't do it!

WHITEFORD: Nonsense! There are a lot of superstitions about every old house.

ILEANA: This isn't a superstition, Ned. It happened once when *I* was a little girl. A man insisted on sleeping there. They found him dead in the morning.

WHITEFORD (*a little shaken*): How did he die?

ILEANA: They don't know. There wasn't a mark on his body. He wasn't shot, or stabbed, or strangled, or poisoned, or hurt in any way. He was just . . . dead.

(*Music up.*)

NARRATOR: Two nights later in the Department of France now known as *Indre-et-Loire* but once called Touraine. The ancient land beloved of Rabelais and Balzac. But now, as the wind moans down the valleys and rain flickers across apple trees and thunder stirs in those haunted hills . . . (*Rain and thunder*) . . . it can bring little comfort to a young man driven in an ancient carriage from the railway station along snakelike roads to *what* destination? Ahead a flash of lightning shows the grey walls and conical slate-roofed towers of a chateau set some distance back from the road. Lights shine from its narrow windows, dimly seen through the rain, as . . .

WHITEFORD: Driver! Coachman!

DRIVER (*dully*): Yes, monsieur?

WHITEFORD: Is that the Chateau d'Azay? Up ahead?

DRIVER: Yes, monsieur. I will take you to the very door, if . . .

WHITEFORD: If what? Why do you cross yourself?

DRIVER: . . . if I am permitted.

WHITEFORD: What should stop you?

DRIVER: Only fear, monsieur. And I am not—*much*—afraid.
(*Howling in distance.*)

WHITEFORD: Listen! What was that?

DRIVER: Only the dogs, monsieur. They keep many dogs, large dogs, at the Chateau d'Azay. You hear them howling?

WHITEFORD: Yes.

DRIVER: Jules Seznac at the inn says it is because two of the dogs died this afternoon. Do dogs mourn their own dead? I don't know.

(*Carriage stops. Dogs howl.*)

DRIVER: Good night, monsieur. And, if one may be permitted a word of advice . . .

WHITEFORD: Well?

DRIVER: Beware of the Tapestry Room.

(*Carriage drives away. Thunder and rain continue.*)

WHITEFORD (*muttering*): If there isn't a bell on this door, there might at least be a knocker. Ah . . . got it!

(*Sound of knocking. Door is opened.* MADAME FLEY, *the housekeeper, has an elderly and not unpleasant voice.*)

MADAME FLEY: *Et alors, monsieur? Vous cherchez . . . ?*

WHITEFORD: *Je cherche le Chateau d'Azay et je . . .*

FLEY (*grimly amused*): Perhaps it would be better if monsieur spoke English. You are Lord Edward Whiteford?

WHITEFORD: Yes.

FLEY: Monsieur is expected. Please to enter.

(*Door closes. Noise of rain ceases. Piano can be heard playing in distance.*)

FLEY: Monsieur's hat and coat?

WHITEFORD: Thank you.

ILEANA: Ned!

WHITEFORD: Ileana!

FLEY (*warningly*): *N'embrasses pas, ma petite! Garde a ton oncle!*

ILEANA: You'd better not kiss me, Ned. Madame Fley says to look out for my uncle.

WHITEFORD: Where is your uncle now?

ILEANA: In the drawing-room. He's playing the piano. Come along.

(*Piano gradually grows louder during their low-voiced speech, indicating approach to the room.*)

WHITEFORD: Ileana, is anything wrong?

ILEANA: Everything's wrong! Two of my dogs were in horrible pain this afternoon. Dr. Saulomon had to put them out with chloroform.

WHITEFORD: You don't think . . . ?

ILEANA: I hope nobody's—practising, that's all. Here we are.

WHITEFORD: Animal-heads on the wall and tiger-skins on the

floor. I say! Who's the little old man with the grey beard, sitting over by the fire?

ILEANA: That's Dr. Saulomon.

WHITEFORD: He's got funny-looking eyes.

ILEANA: He watches and watches and watches. He's an old friend of the family. Sh-h!

(*Sound of piano stops.*)

KOHARY (*affably*): Ah, my young friend. So my niece has anticipated me. Welcome to the Chateau d'Azay.

WHITEFORD: Thank you, Count Kohary.

KOHARY: You must be very wet after your long drive. Go up to the fire and warm yourself. Madame Fley!

FLEY: Yes, monsieur?

KOHARY: Please tell Antoine to take our guest's luggage up to the Tapestry Room.

(*Dogs howl.*)

FLEY (*startled*): The Tapestry Room, monsieur?

KOHARY (*suavely*): That is what I said, Madame Fley.

FLEY: Yes, monsieur.

KOHARY: By an odd coincidence, Lord Edward, Dr. Saulomon and I were just discussing the fate of the last person who slept in the Tapestry Room.

(SAULOMON *has a very old voice, rather thin and quavery, but clear.*)

SAULOMON: This is not good, my friend. This is against my advice. It is the wrong season of the moon.

KOHARY: Moon? But there's no moon tonight. It's raining cats and dogs.

ILEANA: Don't talk about dogs!

SAULOMON: Nevertheless, it is the wrong season of the moon. I say no more.

WHITEFORD (*under his breath*): Cheerful blighter, that doctor!

ILEANA (*under her breath*): Don't do it, Ned! I won't be responsible if they make you do it!

WHITEFORD: But look here, Count Kohary. What *did* happen to the last bloke who slept in the Tapestry Room?

KOHARY: You must not call him a "bloke," young man. He was a very saintly gentleman, the Bishop of Tours. That was some time ago; and Ileana was only fifteen years old. But surely she must remember it.

ILEANA (*shivering*): I remember it!

KOHARY: The Christian Church, said our Bishop, has no use for superstitions. He insisted on sleeping there. I—made him as comfortable as possible. But he was found dead next morning, with the crucifix still in his hand.

(*Dogs howl.*)

WHITEFORD: Was it . . . poison?

SAULOMON (*vehemently*): There was no poison, monsieur!

ILEANA (*under her breath*): It's true, Ned.

(*Few chords strummed on piano.*)

KOHARY: There were just two curious things, young man, in connection with that death. On the mantelpiece was found burning a stick of incense. Ordinary incense. Nothing wrong with it.

WHITEFORD: Yes, sir?

KOHARY: And under the dressing-table—the police found it—was an empty jar of ointment. Now come! Use your wits! A dead man, and some burning incense, and an empty jar of ointment. What do you make of that?

WHITEFORD (*bewildered*): I don't make anything of it. It's crazy!

(*Bang from keys of piano.*)

KOHARY (*through his teeth*): Please do not speak like that!

WHITEFORD: I'm sorry.

SAULOMON: It is *still* the wrong season of the moon.

WHITEFORD (*doggedly*): But what I really meant, sir, was this: Is there any *reason* for this story of death?

KOHARY: Reason?

WHITEFORD: Any legend attached to the room, or something like that?

KOHARY: Yes. There is.

WHITEFORD: Well, sir?

KOHARY (*musingly*): We are a very old family, my friend. Old, and perhaps accursed. When certain of my ancestors moved from Hungary to France in the seventeenth century, they brought certain beliefs with them. The Old Religion.

WHITEFORD (*puzzled*): The Old Religion?

KOHARY: The cult of Diana. The cult of Janus. The cult of freedom and fertility. (*Sharply*) The witch cult, if you prefer.

WHITEFORD: Now look here, sir!

ILEANA (*crying out*): *Must* we talk about this?

KOHARY (*agreeably*): Ah, you smile. When I say the word "witch," you think of some humorous picture on a Hallowe'en card. It was very different in the Middle Ages, believe me. *Then,* my friend, there existed an organized religion which rivalled the Christian Church. There were many to worship unashamed at the Grand Sabbat; to receive all favours from Satan, their master; and to dance forever, joyously, in the red quadrilles of hell.

(*Peal of thunder.*)

WHITEFORD: Yes, but—

KOHARY: Hear me out. Some two hundred years ago an ancestress of mine, Catherine Kohary, was tortured to death in the Tapestry Room for professing the Old Religion. Many persons have not thought it safe to sleep there since. Are you answered?

WHITEFORD: Tell me, sir. Is this some kind of elaborate joke?

KOHARY (*stung*): Joke? The Bishop of Tours did not find it a joke!

SAULOMON: Not a mark on his body. I assure you as a physician, not a mark on his body.

KOHARY: You hear Dr. Saulomon?

WHITEFORD: I hear him.

KOHARY (*kindly*): Understand me, my boy. There's no compulsion in this. If you have not the courage to sleep in that room . . .

WHITEFORD (*not loudly*): Let's get this straight, sir. Do you think I'm afraid to sleep in that room?

KOHARY: Let us just say that I commend your prudence. After thinking the matter over and coming to a more sensible conclusion after—shall I say?—your rather boastful talk at Paris . . .

WHITEFORD (*furious*): I asked you a question, sir. Do you think I'm afraid to sleep in that room?

KOHARY: Frankly I do.

WHITEFORD: Would you like to make a little bet on that?

KOHARY: Bet? What sort of bet?

WHITEFORD: I'll tell you. If I spend the night in this famous room and come out of it alive, will you give your consent to the marriage *immediately?* Tomorrow morning?

KOHARY: Tomorrow morning? Why tomorrow morning?

WHITEFORD: Because I don't think the atmosphere of this house is good for Ileana. That's as plain as I can make it and still be polite. What do you say, Count Kohary?

(*Riffling of piano keys.*)

KOHARY: Very well, my boy. I accept the terms of your wager.

WHITEFORD: There'll be no quibbling or backing out or saying you didn't mean it?

KOHARY: After a few hours in the Tapestry Room, my friend, there will be no need for quibbling.

ILEANA: Don't *do* it, Ned! I *warn* you not to do it. For the love of God; and, for the last time, don't *do* it!

(*Music up.* NARRATOR *speaks with thunder in the background.*)

NARRATOR: High up in the east tower of the Chateau d'Azay, under the conical slate roof, is the circular room hung with faded tapestries. These tapestries move slightly, with uneasy mimic life, to the clamour of the storm outside. Candles burn along the mantelpiece and beside the great four-poster bed. The flames of the candles waver too, as the door opens.

FLEY: This is the Tapestry Room, monsieur.

WHITEFORD: Thank you.

FLEY: *That* is the mantelpiece where the incense burned. *That* is the bed where Monseigneur the Bishop died.

WHITEFORD: Very inviting, isn't it?

FLEY: Will there be anything else that monsieur requires? Some sandwiches? A decanter of whisky?

WHITEFORD: No, thanks. I had a drink with Count Kohary before I came upstairs.

FLEY: *Bien,* monsieur. Monsieur's shaving-water will be brought up in the morning—if he requires it. Good night.

(*Door closes. Sound of thunder.*)

WHITEFORD (*muttering with the rage of nervousness*): Infernal old harpy! Trying to scare a fellow out of his wits just because . . . They've built a good fire, anyway. I didn't realize how cold it was. Temperature must have dropped.

(*Soft knock on door.*)

WHITEFORD (*crying out*): *What's that?*

(*Door opens.*)

ILEANA (*calling softly*): It's me. Ileana. May I come in?

WHITEFORD: No! Get out of here!

ILEANA: That's not very gallant of you.

WHITEFORD: I mean, I don't want *you* to be exposed to whatever it is.

ILEANA: Ned, listen! Are you going to bed, or are you going to sit up all night?

WHITEFORD: I'm going to sit up all night. Naturally.

ILEANA: Then let me sit up with you.

WHITEFORD: No!

ILEANA: Why not?

WHITEFORD: First, because it may be dangerous. Second, because I promised your uncle I'd go through with this alone.

ILEANA (*worried*): I wish you hadn't had that drink with him.

WHITEFORD: He couldn't have done anything to it. *You* poured it.

ILEANA: Yes. That's true. Only . . . *listen!*

(*Sound of slow, heavy footsteps.*)

WHITEFORD: What is it?

ILEANA: It sounded like somebody walking between the walls of this room.

WHITEFORD: By George, it is somebody walking inside the wall. Get behind that tapestry, Ileana! Quick! Hide there.

(*A very long peal of thunder.*)

WHITEFORD: Count Kohary? Where did you come from?

KOHARY: Forgive me, my boy, for seeming to appear out of the wall, and between the tapestries, like Mephisto appearing to Faust. This red dressing-gown perhaps adds to the effect.

WHITEFORD: How did you get here? A passage between the walls?

KOHARY: Exactly. A little device of my ancestors for visiting this room when its occupant was so unmannerly as to bolt the door.

WHITEFORD: The door's not bolted. You could have walked straight through it.

KOHARY: But I could not have done it . . . unobserved.

WHITEFORD: No. Maybe not.

KOHARY: Have you had any other visitors, my boy?

(*Dogs howl.*)

WHITEFORD (*slight pause*): No.

KOHARY: You're quite sure of that?

WHITEFORD: Quite sure.

KOHARY: Then, since nobody saw me come here, I'll just sit down by the fire. Please sit opposite me.

WHITEFORD: Is this the show-down, sir?

KOHARY: I don't understand you.

WHITEFORD: There's got to be a show-down between us. Is that why you're here?

KOHARY: I am here, young man, to explain certain things to you. Will you have a cigarette?

WHITEFORD: I . . .

KOHARY (*amused*): They're not drugged, if that's what you're afraid of. Or *daren't* you have a cigarette?

WHITEFORD: I'll have one.

KOHARY: Good. A light?

WHITEFORD: Thank you.
(*Scratch of match.*)

KOHARY (*leisurely*): When I was discussing the witch cult a while ago, you did not appear to think I meant what I said.

WHITEFORD: Do you want a perfectly frank answer to that?

KOHARY: Yes.

WHITEFORD: I think you're mad enough to mean anything.

KOHARY (*quietly*): What you say, in a sense, is quite true. In an old and inbred family like ours, the mind can crack and the fantasies of witchcraft become as real . . . more real! . . . than the living world. Let me give you an example.

WHITEFORD: Go on.

KOHARY: The saucer on the table beside you is Ming porcelain. It was once owned by Catherine Kohary, a martyr of the Old Religion. Yet you are using it as an ashtray.

WHITEFORD: I beg the witch-lady's pardon. I'll blow off the ash.

KOHARY: A dangerous remark, sir!

WHITEFORD: Sit down, Count Kohary!

KOHARY: Don't you understand that the worship of evil can be as strong and compelling as the worship of good? That the devil can have *his* saints too? That . . . to a sick brain which *knows* but can't help itself . . . you have profaned this room merely by entering it? Therefore you deserve to die?

WHITEFORD: Like the Bishop of Tours?

KOHARY: Exactly.

WHITEFORD: You're not going to tell me the devil killed *him?*

KOHARY: The devil's agent may be flesh and blood, surely?

WHITEFORD (*pouncing*): Then it *was* murder?

KOHARY: Of course it was murder. Murder so cunningly contrived that the police never saw through it.

WHITEFORD: Go on.

KOHARY: I asked you before to use your wits on this problem. Incense was burned in this room. Why?

WHITEFORD: Suppose *you* tell *me*.

KOHARY: Obviously, I think, to conceal something else which would be too easily noticed.

WHITEFORD: To conceal what?

KOHARY: The smell of chloroform.

(*Thunder.*)

WHITEFORD: Chloroform?

KOHARY: Yes. A drug not well understood by laymen. Dr. Saulomon was using chloroform this afternoon to dispose of some dogs.

WHITEFORD: So I've heard.

KOHARY: Dr. Saulomon is old. And—forgetful.

WHITEFORD (*a little unsteadily*): You mean . . . chloroform could be stolen?

KOHARY: It *could* be, easily. Now suppose . . . just suppose! . . . I take a pad saturated with chloroform. I place it over the mouth and nostrils of a man already sleeping or drugged, so that he gets no other air.

WHITEFORD (*unsteadily*): Wait a minute! That . . . won't do!

KOHARY: Why not?

WHITEFORD (*with an effort*): Chloroform burns and blisters when it touches the skin. You'd leave marks.

KOHARY: Not at all, my friend. Not at all! If I first covered the mouth and nostrils with some substance like . . .

WHITEFORD (*crying out*): Ointment!

KOHARY (*agreeably*): Ah, we're waking up.

WHITEFORD (*dizzily*): I . . . I . . .

KOHARY: Now observe what follows. In a few seconds, unconsciousness. In two minutes, three minutes—death.

WHITEFORD: Certain death. Yes.

KOHARY: But chloroform is volatile. It evaporates. There is no trace in the stomach, since nothing has been swallowed. Delay your post-mortem for twenty-four hours—a very easy matter in these country districts—and no trace remains in the blood. Murder without a mark, my friend. Murder without a mark.

WHITEFORD (*heavily*): You can't do it, Count Kohary! There's just one thing you're forgetting.

KOHARY: What's that?

WHITEFORD: *I'm* not sleeping. And I'm not drugged.

KOHARY: Oh, yes, you are.

(*Thunder.*)

WHITEFORD: In—the cigarette?

KOHARY: No. In the drink you had with me.

WHITEFORD: What . . . was it?

KOHARY: Morphine. You've had enough to put three men to sleep. Try to get up!

WHITEFORD: I'll try! And I'll do it!

(*Crash and clang of metal.*)

KOHARY: You see? You've knocked over the fire-irons. You'd have been in the fire yourself if I hadn't caught you.

WHITEFORD (*dizzily*): Take your hands off me! I won't go under! I won't! If I could reach that bell-pull . . .

KOHARY: You can't, my friend. You're only wasting what breath you have left. Didn't I tell you not to trust surface appearances? Didn't I warn you what shapes might lie behind the mask you saw in public? But you had no faith in the religion of our fathers; you had no faith in these outworn superstitions; and you wouldn't take warning.

WHITEFORD (*yelling*): You lunatic, do you think I ever trusted you for a second? I knew what you were going to try; only I thought you couldn't get away with it. *You* killed the Bishop of Tours! And now you're going to kill me!

KOHARY (*amazed*): One moment! You don't think . . . you don't think *I* am trying to kill you?

(*Thunder.*)

WHITEFORD: Why bother to pretend now?

KOHARY: You don't think *I* killed the Bishop of Tours? Or had anything at all to do with this? I had reckoned on stupidity, but hardly such stupidity as this. You damned young fool, I'm not trying to kill you. I'm trying to *save* you!

WHITEFORD: To—to save me?

KOHARY: Dr. Saulomon!

SAULOMON (*off*): Yes, *Monsieur le Comte?*

KOHARY: Come out from behind the secret door, now. Come out, and be my witness.

SAULOMON: Yes, monsieur. I shall always guard the family honor, even when I guess how men die.

KOHARY: This young man apparently thinks I have been talking about *myself*. Now, tell me, Doctor, am I, in the popular parlance, insane?

SAULOMON: Heaven forbid, monsieur! I have never known a saner man.

WHITEFORD: I can't stand this much longer! The drug's taken hold. I can't see straight any longer. I . . .

KOHARY: Have you any notion, Lord Edward, why I invited you to this house?

WHITEFORD: No.

KOHARY: Would you have believed me, my friend, if I had merely *told* you? Oh, no. Youth is too wise, too brash, too trusting. If I were to convince you of anything, I had to bring you here and show you.

WHITEFORD: Show me . . . what?

SAULOMON (*alarmed*): *Monsieur le Comte,* there is someone behind the tapestries! I saw them move!

WHITEFORD: It's nobody who can hurt you. It's only . . .

KOHARY: It is only—Ileana. Is that what you would say?

WHITEFORD: Yes.

KOHARY: Then, in the black second before unconsciousness, ask yourself these questions. Why have I kept Ileana so carefully guarded from the world? Why, at a fancy-dress ball, did I object to the costume of a medieval witch? Whose dogs were poisoned so that chloroform should be brought here? *Who poured you the drink drugged with morphine?*

WHITEFORD (*screaming*): In the name of God, what are you trying to tell me?

KOHARY: It was Ileana! She has been hopelessly insane for more than ten years!

(*A woman's laughter, high and shrill and maniacal, mingles with thunder and the music.*)

January 19, 1943.

Can a story about a swimming pool in the basement of a country house be a genuine shocker? As the narrator points out, you won't realize how shocking until the final speech. Longtime readers of Carr's works will find one aspect of the play to be reminiscent: he borrowed his own method from an earlier short story of making a weapon disappear, but otherwise the play is entirely different . . . and terrifying.

The Dragon in the Pool

THE CHARACTERS:

Andrew Prentice	A businessman
Tony Prentice	His stepson
Mary Prentice	His daughter
Philip Lockwood	Her fiancé
Chief Inspector Fielding	Of Scotland Yard
Renfield	The butler

Setting: An English country house, early 1940s.

NARRATOR: Tonight's tale is rather an ugly story—yes, distinctly an ugly story—though you may not realize how ugly until the final speech. It has caused me many a chuckle as I ponder on the ways of women. Let us listen as Mary Prentice speaks for herself about a curious crime and an even more curious retribution.

(*Music up.* MARY PRENTICE *is in her late twenties; she has a quiet, self-controlled voice.*)

MARY: Swimming pools, you know, can be very dangerous places. *We* have a swimming pool in the basement of our house in the country. But of course you know that. My father built the pool when he made all that money on the stock exchange, two or three years before my father . . . died.

(PHILIP LOCKWOOD *is in his early thirties, with a reserved but very worried manner.*)

PHIL: Steady, Mary. Take it easy.

MARY (*plaintively*): But I *want* to tell them about it, Phil. I want to tell them why swimming pools can be very dangerous places.

PHIL: You're not *obliged* to say anything, Mary. Do you understand that?

MARY (*unheeding*): My father, of course, didn't die in the swimming pool. But that pool is the answer to the whole mystery. It's a little underground room with walls made out of looking-glasses and mosaic tile on the roof. Tony . . . that's my step-brother, the man you're concerned with . . . Tony was very fond of that pool. He used to go for a swim there every morning before breakfast. I can see him yet, standing on the edge of the diving board in that arrogant way of his and saying . . .

TONY (*on echo to indicate flashback*): I always begin with a swan dive. Watch this!

(*Creak and snap of diving board. Splash.*)

MARY: . . . and the hollow echo of the splash, and spray against the mirror-walls, and the water disturbed so that the pattern of white tiles in the pool grew all blurred. Very clear, that water is. *Very* clear.

PHIL: I tell you Mary, you can't do any good by talking like this. Tony—

MARY: It's all over, isn't it, Phil?

PHIL: Yes. All over.

MARY: But I want to tell about yesterday, and the horrible thing that happened by the pool. I want you to see and feel that underground room, with the lights shining on the unsteady water, and the close warm atmosphere, and the sense of dread that's been over the whole house ever since my father died. (*Slight pause*) I hadn't slept very well, the night before. You'll understand that, I think, when you hear what happened. About half an hour before breakfast I went to Phil's room—Phil was staying with us—and knocked at the door. Phil had just finished dressing, and I asked him to come along with me. There was another person too who'd just arrived from London. I didn't tell them, either of them, what was in my mind. We went downstairs. . . . Do you remember, Phil?

PHIL (*grimly*): I remember.

MARY: Tony hadn't gone into the pool yet.

PHIL: He was just coming out of the little dressing-room, in a bright-striped beach robe and sandals. (*With intensity*) I always hated that infernal gigolo look of his, with the rolling eyes and teeth like a dental advertisement. But I never expected . . . Lord knows I never expected . . .

(*Music up, fading into* Tony's *voice, which is one of breeziness and patronage. Scene on echo.*)

Tony (*surprised*): Good morning, Mary. *Good* morning, my little sister.

Mary: Good morning, Tony.

Tony: You're up rather early, aren't you? Didn't you have a good night?

Mary (*tensely*): Do I *look* as though I'd had a good night?

Tony (*kindly*): Frankly, old girl, you look like the wrath of God.

Mary: Maybe I have reason to.

Tony: Come and have a dip in the pool. *That'll* blow the cobwebs out of your head.

Mary: No, thanks, Tony. Not this morning.

Tony: What about you, Phil? Plenty of spare bathing costumes. Climb into one and I'll race you twice the length of the pool.

Phil: If you don't mind, Tony, I think I'll give it a miss too.

Tony: All right, all right! I was only trying to be friendly. (*With sudden pettishness*) I can't think what the devil's the matter with you two!

Mary: No, Tony?

Tony: No! If you're going to get married, why don't you *get* married instead of moping about the house like a couple of moonstruck kids? Why *did* you come down here at this hour of the morning, if it wasn't to go swimming?

Phil: I don't know what this is all about, Tony. But I think . . .

Tony: Well?

Phil: I think Mary wants to have a word with you.

Tony: Oh? About what?

Mary: About my father's death.

Tony (*wearily impatient*): Now look here, old girl . . .

Mary: I'm so serious about it, Tony, that I've asked a certain person here to meet you. (*Calling*) Mr. Fielding! Mr. Fielding! Will you come in, please?

(Fielding *is in his late forties, with a deep, slow-speaking voice, smooth and almost affable yet faintly sinister: a semi-educated voice with a certain amount of false deference.*)

Fielding (*off, but approaching*): Just as you say, miss. Very nice swimming pool you've got here. Very pleasant house altogether. Yes, indeed.

TONY (*under his breath*): Here! Who's the heavy-set blighter with the wicked eye?

MARY: This, Tony, is Mr. Fielding. Chief Inspector Fielding. From Scotland Yard.

TONY: Scotland Yard?

MARY (*quickly*): Does that scare you, Tony?

TONY (*coolly*): No, old girl, I can't say it does. But I don't understand it!

FIELDING (*fading on*): I don't mind admitting, sir, that I don't exactly understand it myself.

TONY: May I ask, Chief Inspector Fielding, just what in blazes you're *doing* here?

FIELDING: I'm here, sir, because the young lady invited me.

TONY (*startled*): Invited you?

FIELDING: She wrote to the Assistant Commissioner for the Criminal Investigation Department, and said she'd tell us the whole truth about the Prentice murder . . .

PHIL: Mary!

FIELDING: . . . if we'd send somebody down here at exactly half-past eight in the morning. I don't understand this "half-past-eight" business. But here I am. And if the young lady *has* got something to tell us—?

MARY: I've got a great deal to tell you, Chief Inspector.

TONY: Are you sure that's wise, old girl?

MARY: Wise, Tony? How?

TONY (*coolly*): Well! If you intend confessing to the murder . . .

MARY (*amazed*): Confessing to the murder? Saying I killed my own father?

TONY: Isn't that what you're doing?

MARY: You know it's not, Tony Prentice!

TONY: But you must be accusing somebody, old girl. And you certainly can't be accusing *me*. On the night the poor old governor died . . . (*emotionally*) . . . and Lord knows he was the best father a bloke could ask for . . . but on that night—

MARY: He wasn't your father, Tony Prentice. He was your stepfather.

TONY (*unheeding*): On that night, I was away in London. I accounted to the police for every second of my time. I've got an alibi as big as a house. You certainly don't dispute that?

MARY: No. I don't dispute it.

TONY: Then would you mind holding my beach robe, old girl? I've had enough of this! I'm going in for a swim.

MARY (*quickly*): *I* shouldn't dive into that pool, Tony.

TONY: No? Why not?

MARY: Because it might be dangerous.

TONY: Dangerous?

MARY: At least until you hear what I've got to say.

FIELDING (*insistently*): But that's just the point, miss. Speaking as a police officer, I still don't understand this. What *have* you got to say?

TONY (*sarcastically*): Bravo, Chief Inspector!

FIELDING: Your father, if I've got the facts straight, was killed upstairs in the library . . .

MARY: Yes, that's what I want to tell you. He died on the night of the sixteenth of July, during a summer thunderstorm. Please remember that thunderstorm.

PHIL (*puzzled*): Look here, my dear. What the devil has the thunderstorm got to do with it?

TONY: Hear the voice of sanity! Hear the voice of good old Phil Lockwood!

MARY (*fiercely*): Will you listen to me, Tony?

TONY: All right, old girl. I should hate to spoil your fun.

MARY: It had been very warm, before the storm broke. Aside from the servants, the only other persons in the house were myself and Phil here. Tony was in London.

FIELDING: I know all that, miss. But—

MARY: After dinner, about nine o'clock, I was in the library with my father. He—he said he wanted to speak to me alone. Have you seen the library, Chief Inspector?

FIELDING: No, miss. I wasn't in charge of the case. But—

MARY: It's a big old-fashioned room with French windows opening out on a terrace. My father was standing by the big table in the middle of the room. He hadn't been well, and he was looking ghastly. He'd said something about taking his medicine. I saw the light shining down on the pitcher of water, and the tumbler with the soda water, and the little medicine bottle. Then the storm broke. . . .

(*Music up, fading to sounds of thunder and rain.*)

(ANDREW PRENTICE *is only in his fifties, but he has the elderly voice of ill-health and despair; it overshadows his essential kindliness.*)

PRENTICE: Mary! Please!

MARY (*off*): Yes, father?

PRENTICE: Come away from those windows. What are you doing at the windows?

MARY: I'm only closing them, father.

PRENTICE (*petulantly*): Never mind the windows, my dear. Come here and sit down.

MARY (*fading on*): Yes, of course, if you insist. (*Bursting out*) Father, what on earth *is* the matter?

PRENTICE (*grimly*): So *you* know there's something wrong. I imagine everybody does.

MARY: I know you're ill, that's all! And not yourself! And—

PRENTICE: Sit down, Mary.

MARY: Yes, father.

PRENTICE (*after a pause*): I've been doing a lot of thinking recently, Mary. And in the middle of the night—two, three, four o'clock—that's when it's worst.

MARY: Thinking—about what?

PRENTICE: About you and Tony.

MARY: Well, father?

PRENTICE (*reflectively*): I suppose deep down in his heart what a man wants most is the respect of his children. When he loses that respect, one of two things happens. Either he hates his children, or he hates himself. Well, God knows I don't hate you!

MARY (*crying out*): Father, what *are* you talking about?

PRENTICE (*flatly*): I'm finished, Mary. I'm cleaned out. I'm broke. Wait! Don't speak for a minute!

MARY (*fiercely restrained*): Very well.

PRENTICE: A fine house, a staff of servants, two or three motor-cars. And in a month or two—nothing.

MARY (*still restrained*): I see.

PRENTICE: If a man can't give his children success, what can he give them? What else has he got to offer? At least, that's what Tony says.

MARY (*with hatred*): That's what Tony says, is it?

PRENTICE (*shaken*): What's wrong, Mary? Why do you clench your hands like that?

MARY: I was just thinking that I hate the very ground Tony walks on!

PRENTICE (*querulously*): You mustn't talk like that, Mary.

MARY: Don't *you* ever dislike him at all?

PRENTICE (*hesitating*): The boy is utterly cold-blooded. I admit that.

MARY: Yes. And yet you seem to prefer him to . . . to . . .

PRENTICE: To my own daughter, were you going to say?

MARY: Well! Yes!

PRENTICE: Tony's mother was my first wife. I was very fond of her. I . . . anyway, that's beside the question. The point is, my dear, that the boy's right. He's absolutely right!

MARY: *Is* he right, father?

PRENTICE: To admit you're a failure after all your fine show—to be cleaned out of everything you've worked for—just because you're not quite as clever as the other fellow . . .

MARY: Tony's goaded you about that, hasn't he?

PRENTICE: Mary! Please! Let me finish!

MARY: Very well, father.

PRENTICE: I've never talked straight out to you before. I—I couldn't! But there's one thing I'm bound to mention now.

MARY: Oh? What's that?

PRENTICE: My life insurance. You'd be very well taken care of, both you *and* Tony, if anything ever happened to me. (*Long roll of thunder.*)

PRENTICE (*mildly*): What's the matter, my dear? It's only thunder.

MARY: It wasn't the thunder that made me jump. I was just wondering what you were thinking.

PRENTICE (*drily*): Not, I'm certain, what *you* were thinking.

MARY: No?

PRENTICE: If you were thinking, my dear, that I might kill myself . . .

MARY: Well?

PRENTICE (*wryly amused*): Get the idea out of your head. My life insurance policies all have a suicide clause. But suppose —mind, I only say suppose—somebody killed me? Suppose some kindly enemy should turn up . . . tonight, even . . . and . . . (*Breaking off*) Careful, Mary!

MARY (*dazed*): Careful? Of what?

PRENTICE (*pettishly*): That water pitcher, my dear, is very expensive glass. Don't knock it off the table! And mind my medicine bottle!

MARY: I'm sorry, father. (*Frantically*) But you've got to stop talking this horrible nonsense!

PRENTICE: *Is* it nonsense?

MARY: You haven't got any enemies.

PRENTICE: Oh, yes, I have.

MARY: Who?

PRENTICE: Someone, I think, whom you might not suspect. A kindly enemy, to cut my throat or put a bullet into me, and solve the whole problem.

MARY (*breathlessly*): Father, listen to me! You're not well. Do you think it *matters* whether you've lost this money or not?

PRENTICE: Not to you, perhaps. You'll be marrying Phil Lockwood, and Phil's a good, steady-going fellow. But Tony! And your Aunt Hester in London!

MARY (*bitterly*): Tony! Always Tony!

PRENTICE (*earnestly*): Don't you see, Mary, it would be the best way out?

MARY: It wouldn't! I tell you it wouldn't!

PRENTICE: I never thought I should pray for death. But I'm praying for it now. If someone should creep up this minute, and fire a shot through one of those French windows . . .

MARY: Was that why you wanted the windows left open?

PRENTICE: I should be afraid, of course. I'm a good deal of a coward. But if this murderer *were* to come through the window, or to knock at the hall door over there . . .

(*Sharp knocking on door.*)

MARY (*crying out*): Who's there?

(*Door opens.*)

PHIL (*off, surprised*): Great Scott, what's the matter with you two? It's only me.

MARY: Phil!

PRENTICE: Come in, Phil. Come in. Mary and I have just . . . finished talking.

MARY: We have *not* finished talking! Father, listen to me!

PRENTICE (*unheeding*): And, as a matter of fact, I was just sending Mary away.

MARY: Sending me away?

PRENTICE: Yes. I've got to take my medicine.

(*Thunder.*)

PHIL (*approaching*): It must have been a very interesting talk, whatever it was. Do you realize, sir, that the windows are all standing wide open?

MARY: He realizes it, Phil! And you've got to help me! He's got a crazy idea that . . .

PRENTICE (*very sharply*): Mary!

MARY: Yes, father?

PRENTICE: What I said a moment ago was for yourself alone. Do you understand that?

MARY: No! Not until I make sure you don't mean it! You can't mean it!

PRENTICE: I mean, at least, that I'm sending you out of here. I'm going to take you by the shoulders, like this . . . I'm going to march you across to the door, like this . . . Come along, Phil! . . . I'm going to put you out into the hall, like this . . . (*More lightly*) And I propose, like a stern parent, to close the door in your face. Good night, Mary.

MARY (*desperately*): Will you *listen* to me for a minute?

PRENTICE (*a little off*): Good night, Mary.

(*Door closes. Slight pause. A grandfather clock is heard ticking through the next scene.*)

PHIL (*quietly*): All right, Mary. Let's hear it.

MARY: Hear what?

PHIL: There was the very devil to pay in there, and you know it. (*Rather bitterly*) I'm not very inspired, I admit. I'm the good old dependable cab-horse. But I've got eyes and ears.

MARY: Could you hear what we were saying?

PHIL: No. I didn't need to hear it. We're all alone in the hall here. Tell me.

MARY: Father thinks . . . (*Breaking off*) We're not alone here, either! (*Calling*) Who's there?

PHIL: Where? I don't see anybody.

MARY: Down there. Past the grandfather clock.

PHIL (*almost amused*): That's only Renfield, Mary. You're not afraid of your own butler, are you?

MARY: I don't know. I'm afraid of everybody. (*Calling*) Renfield!

(RENFIELD *is a typical upper-class servant.*)

RENFIELD (*off*): Yes, miss?

MARY: Come here a moment, please.

RENFIELD (*fading on*): Yes, miss.

MARY: Did you—want anything in particular?

RENFIELD (*surprised*): No, miss. I saw Mr. Prentice come with you to the door of the library, and I wondered if *he* might want anything. (*Hesitating*) Have I given offence in any way?

MARY: No. I'm sorry. It was only my nerves.

PHIL: We're all a bit on edge, I'm afraid.

MARY: The clock sounds as loud as Doomsday; we seem to be waiting for something; and every minute, while this storm is going on . . . (*Very heavy crash of thunder*) Listen! What was that?

PHIL: It was only the thunder, Mary.

MARY: Phil, I'll swear it was something more than thunder! And it . . . it came from the library.

PHIL: Nonsense!

RENFIELD (*a little agitated*): If you'll excuse me, sir, I think Miss Mary is right. It sounds to me like . . .

PHIL: Like what?

RENFIELD: Well, sir, like something heavy falling over on the floor.

MARY: Phil, open the door! Quick!

PHIL: I don't know what's on your mind, Mary. I don't know what you're afraid of. But, whatever you do, don't upset yourself just because a lamp or something blows over in a thunderstorm. There's absolutely nothing to be alarmed about! There's absolutely nothing to be . . .

MARY (*screaming*): Did you hear what I said? Open the *door!*

PHIL: All right, then! Take it easy.

(*Door opens. Slight pause.*)

MARY (*calling*): Father!

PHIL (*a little puzzled*): He's not here, Mary. He must have gone out by one of the windows.

RENFIELD (*grimly*): Excuse me, sir, but I think Mr. Prentice *is* here.

PHIL: Where?

RENFIELD: On the other side of the big table and the telephone stand. He's lying on his back. You can just see the edge of his shoe where the light strikes it, and . . .

MARY (*crying out*): Father!

PHIL: Mary! Don't run over there! Give me your hand. Now walk slowly, with me, and keep your head. Slowly now—round the edge of the table—and . . .

MARY: There's blood running down from the side of his mouth!

PHIL (*very sharply*): Mary! Listen to me!

MARY: Yes, Phil?

PHIL: Turn your back and look at the other side of the room. Do you hear me? Turn your back and look at the other side of the room! Renfield and I will attend to this. (*As though turning round*) Where are you, Renfield?

RENFIELD: Here, sir. But I think—

PHIL: Yes. I'm afraid it's too late.

MARY: He moved just then! I *saw* him move!

PHIL: That was a convulsion, Mary. There's nothing you can do. It's all over.

MARY: How did he . . . ?

PHIL (*slight pause*): He's been stabbed through the chest with a big wide-bladed knife.

RENFIELD (*shaken*): If you'll excuse me, sir, I don't think I want to look at it any longer. But I must say I've been rather expecting this.

MARY (*quickly*): You've been expecting—what?

RENFIELD: He's been depressed, miss. Very depressed. You couldn't help noticing it. If Mr. Prentice *has* killed himself . . .

PHIL: He didn't kill himself. He couldn't have killed himself.

RENFIELD: Couldn't have killed himself, sir? Why not?

PHIL: Because there's no weapon. Look at the wound, man!

RENFIELD (*firmly*): Thank you, sir, no!

PHIL: The knife, whatever it was, has been taken away. What's more . . . look here!

MARY (*steadily*): I don't mind looking, Phil.

PHIL: Somebody took a handkerchief, and wiped the blood off the knife, and then dropped that handkerchief beside him. Afterwards the murderer got away . . .

MARY: Through one of the French windows.

PHIL: I suppose he must have. He certainly didn't come out the door past us . . .

RENFIELD: No, sir. *I* can testify to that.

PHIL: And there's nobody here now. (*Brooding*) All the same, though, the whole thing's damned queer. It's pouring with rain outside, and yet this carpet looks as dry as a bone. You'd think anybody who came in would leave marks.

MARY: *That* doesn't matter, Phil. There's a porch roof outside. Anyway . . . father expected it.

PHIL: He expected what?

MARY: He said somebody was going to kill him. He was waiting for it.

PHIL: But that's the most impossible part of the whole thing! Your father hadn't an enemy in the world.

MARY: Oh, yes, he had. He told me so.

PHIL (*quickly*): What enemy?

MARY: He wouldn't tell me that. He said it was somebody I mightn't suspect.

(*Telephone rings stridently.*)

PHIL: Steady, Mary! There's nothing to be alarmed about when a telephone rings.

MARY: Isn't there, Phil? I think there is. Renfield!

RENFIELD: Yes, miss?

MARY: Let *me* answer that, please. I'm almost sure I can guess who it is.

RENFIELD: Just as you like, miss.

MARY (*softly vicious*): Hello, Tony. Hello, Tony darling. It *is* Tony speaking, isn't it?

TONY (*on filter*): By George, old girl, you must be a ruddy mind-reader!

MARY: Sometimes I think I can read your mind straight through. Where are you now, Tony? Just tell me that. Where are you now?

TONY: I'm in the grill-room of the Isis Hotel, old girl. If you listen closely, you can hear the orchestra. I'm with Barbara Lane and Jim Preston and Bob Meadows; and I've been here for the past hour. Wonderful party! Wonderful champagne! Wonderful evening! (*Laughs*) How's every little thing at home?

(*Thunder. Music up, fading to the swimming pool scene.*)

MARY: And that's all there was to it, Chief Inspector Fielding. That's what I've brought you down here to tell you. (*Sharply*) Tony! Aren't *you* paying any attention to this?

TONY: I'm sorry, old girl. I was only throwing the rubber horse into the swimming pool. (*Slight splash*) There!

MARY: You just aren't interested, are you, Tony?

TONY: I'm sorry, old girl, but it's all ancient history. The governor's dead.

MARY: Oh, yes. He's dead.

TONY: And I don't see the good of raking it all over again. What do *you* say, Chief Inspector?

FIELDING: Well, sir, I'm bound to say I agree with you. (*Rather exasperated*) Look here, miss; I know all these details. We've been over and over 'em at the Yard. Why do you want to go through the whole thing again?

MARY: Because I was hoping—when you heard *all* the evidence— you might see the essential clue.

FIELDING: Essential clue, miss? What clue?

MARY: The clue that tells us how my father really died. (*Knife-chord*) What's the matter *now*, Tony? (*Pouncing*) Why are you looking like that?

TONY: There's nothing the matter with me.

MARY: Look at his face, Chief Inspector! Look at his face, Phil!

PHIL: I see it!

MARY: He's taking off his beach robe in a very leisurely way, isn't he? He's going to do one of his famous swan dives off the springboard, just to show us he doesn't care. But his face is as white as the tiles down there under that water, and he's scared out of his wits because he *knows* I've guessed!

FIELDING: Guessed what?

MARY: Ask Tony.

PHIL: Look here, Mary; are you accusing Tony of causing your father's death?

MARY: Yes, Phil. I am.

PHIL: But that's impossible!

TONY: If I were you, Mary, I should be very, very careful. You might get your silly little neck wrung for talking poisonous nonsense like that. When somebody stabbed the old man, I was in London in a restaurant full of people. *Is* that true, or isn't it?

MARY: Oh, yes. It's true enough.

FIELDING: Then what are you getting at, miss?

MARY: He's morally guilty of my father's death. As guilty as though he'd held the dagger. Don't you see the trick even yet? Any of you?

PHIL: No. What trick?

MARY: My father committed suicide. But it was made to look like murder, so that we could collect the insurance money. And Tony showed him how to do it.

TONY (*suddenly hoarse*): Mary! Don't be a blasted fool!

MARY: I've touched you *now*, haven't I?

TONY: She doesn't know what she's talking about!

MARY: Oh, yes, I do.

FIELDING: Go on, miss.

MARY: It was very easy, wasn't it, Tony? He was old; he was ill; he was sick with worry. You persuaded him he'd be better off dead, and showed him a fool-proof way of cheating the insurance company.

PHIL: Wait a minute. This is all very well, but it won't do!

MARY: Why not?

PHIL: Because there wasn't any weapon.

MARY: Yes, there was.

PHIL: I searched the room; the police searched the room; and there wasn't any weapon. Your father surely couldn't have hidden it afterwards.

MARY: No, he didn't hide it.

PHIL: Then what *did* he do?

MARY: After he'd stabbed himself, he had just strength enough left to clean the blood off that knife with a handkerchief. Then he put the knife down in plain sight. But nobody ever saw it.

PHIL: He put it down in plain sight? But nobody ever saw it?

MARY: That's right, Phil.

FIELDING (*heavily*): Look here, miss. I don't want to suggest you're stark, staring mad, but are you talking about an invisible knife?

MARY: Yes. A quite literally invisible knife.

FIELDING (*desperately*): But listen, miss! The blade that killed Mr. Prentice was five inches long and a quarter of an inch thick. What sort of knife *would* be invisible if you put it down in plain sight?

MARY: A knife made of ordinary plain glass . . .

PHIL: *What?*

MARY: A knife made of ordinary plain glass, placed in a glass pitcher of water on the table. You haven't forgotten that glass pitcher of water, have you? Father was desperately anxious I shouldn't knock it over. Because . . .

PHIL: I think I begin to see!

MARY: You can make a glass knife with the crudest cutting tools. And glass is murderous stuff. After my father stabbed himself, the knife was wiped clean and dropped into that pitcher. Everyone who came into the room looked straight through the knife in the water and never saw it.

PHIL: And afterwards?

MARY: Afterwards, of course, Tony removed the evidence. (*Fiercely*) *Didn't you, Tony?*

TONY: You can't prove that, old girl. You can't prove a single blasted word of it.

MARY: Of course I can't prove it. I only guessed it a few days ago when I wondered why the knife was cleaned. (*With longing*) I can't prove it, Tony. That's why I want you to confess it.

TONY: Have you gone out of your mind?

MARY (*insistently*): Confess it, Tony!

TONY (*alarmed*): Keep away from me! You're mad! Do you hear?

MARY: Confess it, Tony! They won't hang you or anything. You'll only lose the money; the money you've worked for and schemed for and killed your best friend for. That's why I'm giving you a last chance to . . .

TONY: I've had just about enough of this! It's all a pack of lies, and you can't prove any different. I don't want to hear any more about it! I'm going for my swim. Stand away from that diving board!

MARY: You always begin with a swan dive, don't you, Tony?

TONY (*fiercely*): Yes! I always begin with a swan dive. Watch this!

FIELDING (*suddenly warned*): Wait a minute, young fellow. I was just wondering . . .

MARY (*ecstatically*): It's too late now, Chief Inspector!

(*Creak and snap of diving board. Sharp splash. Then, bursting out, hollow noises: gurgles of a scream bubbling up from underwater, mixed with thrashing as of a body in agony.*)

PHIL: What in God's name is happening to him?

FIELDING (*galvanized*): Lend a hand, sir! We've got to get him out!

MARY: You can't get him out, Chief Inspector.

PHIL: The water in the pool is turning red. He's thrashing like a shark with a harpoon through its middle. He's twisted up in agony as though . . .

MARY: Can't you guess, both of you, what is happening to him?
(*Music up strongly, fading under as* MARY *speaks again.*)

MARY (*quietly*): I arranged it, of course, the night before. I drained the water out of the pool first of all. I dug the cement from between two of the white tiles, and fitted in a long narrow stake of sharpened glass with its point upwards. Then I ran water into the pool again. Tony couldn't see the glass stake in the water, any more than we could see the blade when my father died. I've never forgotten the look of Tony's back muscles when he dived in, and the glass point ran through his stomach, and he tried to twist round and look up at us through the pink water just after the blood came out of his mouth. That's all I have to tell you people here at Scotland Yard, either to the Assistant Commissioner, or the man who's taking this down in shorthand, or even poor Phil who came along with me. Tony as good as killed my father, and I think he deserved to die. But swimming pools, I repeat, can be very dangerous places.
(*Music up.*)

February 3, 1944.

For people who heard the American or the British version, "The Dead Sleep Lightly" remains one of John Dickson Carr's most memorable accomplishments. With its shuddery atmosphere, its seemingly inexplicable events, and its rational conclusion, it is Carr at his finest. The American version begins in a cemetery with the minister intoning "ashes to ashes, dust to dust." When the play was broadcast in Britain, Carr lengthened the script by a third to include Dr. Fell and Superintendent Hadley.

The Dead Sleep Lightly

THE CHARACTERS:

Dr. Gideon Fell — The detective
Hoskins — His manservant
George Pendleton — A publisher
Pamela Bennett — His secretary
Mrs. Tancred — His housekeeper
Wilmot — His chauffeur
Superintendent Hadley — Of Scotland Yard
Mary Ellen Kimball — A voice
Taxi Driver
Telephone Operator

Setting: London, 1933.

NARRATOR: It was dark that night too. Very dark. A gusty March evening ten years ago in London. There was peace; there was security; and no living thing could harm you. But a black wind whistled that night in the narrow streets off the Strand, and flapped at the shutters and growled in the chimneys, and penetrated even into the snug book-lined study up two flights of stairs. There in the great padded armchair before the fire, sat Dr. Gideon Fell. His face had grown even ruddier in the heat of the fire. His several chins folded out over his collar. Cigar ash was spilled down the mountainous ridges of his waistcoat. His eyeglasses, on the wide black ribbon, had become a trifle lopsided. Doubtless he was deep in thought over some difficult problem, since . . .

(*As the voice fades, there are several long and impressive snores. Door opens as* HOSKINS *approaches.*)

HOSKINS: Dr. Fell, sir! Wake up! Dr. Fell!

DR. FELL (*at end of a snore, starting*): Eh? What's that?

HOSKINS: Begging your pardon, sir, but *will* you wake up?

DR. FELL (*with dignity*): Yes, of course; I was merely concentrating. What is it?

HOSKINS: There's a lunatic downstairs, sir.

DR. FELL: A *what?*

HOSKINS: A lunatic, sir.

DR. FELL: Then what's wrong, my good Hoskins? What ails you? Why don't you show him up?

HOSKINS: Are you sure you *want* to see him, sir?

DR. FELL: That depends. What sort of a lunatic is he?

HOSKINS: He's a big, fine-looking gent, about fifty. Got a limousine outside. But he's shaking all over, and near purple in the face. I don't like the look of him.

DR. FELL: Did he give any name?

HOSKINS: Well, sir, he started to take out a card case. But his fingers shook so much that he spilled the cards all over the floor. Then he scooped up the lot and put 'em back in his pocket again. I think he said "Pendleton" or something like that.

DR. FELL (*ruminating*): Pendleton. That wouldn't be George Pendleton, the publisher?

HOSKINS: I dunno, sir.

DR. FELL: Mr. George Pendleton, Hoskins, is a very celebrated and successful man. What he should be doing at *my* humble door . . . Ask him to come up, will you?

HOSKINS (*rapidly, under his breath*): Cripes, sir, I don't need to. 'Ere 'e is.

(*Door opens.* PENDLETON *has an authoritative and pompous voice, the voice of a man used to getting his own way. Just now he has himself in hand, but he is badly frightened.*)

PENDLETON (*huskily*): I beg your pardon. Am I addressing Dr. Gideon Fell?

DR. FELL: At your service, sir. Mr. Pendleton?

PENDLETON: Yes. I followed your servant up. That dark hall downstairs . . . (*Correcting himself quickly*) I mean, I hope you'll excuse my intrusion at this time of the night. I mean . . .

DR. FELL: Steady, man! Don't trip over anything. Here, come up to the fire. It's a cold night.

PENDLETON (*fervently*): It is, it is!

DR. FELL: Hoskins, take Mr. Pendleton's hat and coat. Now draw up a chair.

PENDLETON: Tell me, Doctor: there's no clay in this house, is there?

DR. FELL: Clay?

PENDLETON: Clay soil. And gravel. Of the sort you often find in . . . graveyards.

HOSKINS (*under his breath*): 'Ere! Stop a bit!

DR. FELL: That will be all, Hoskins. You may go.

HOSKINS (*unwillingly*): Very good, sir.

(*Door closes.*)

PENDLETON: I thought I stepped on some clay and gravel as I was coming upstairs. Perhaps a trick of the imagination.

DR. FELL: It certainly must have been, unless Hoskins is an even worse housekeeper than I think he is.

PENDLETON: You see, Doctor . . . I went to a funeral yesterday.

DR. FELL: You've lost someone?

PENDLETON: No, no, no! It was only a fellow club-member. A lot of us went to the funeral in a body, as a mark of respect. (*Pompously*) I'm a busy man, Doctor, but I find it pays to keep up the little social duties like that. Business, with the right personal touch: that's how I've got on in the world, if you don't mind my saying so.

DR. FELL: I see. And on this particular social occasion . . . ?

PENDLETON (*startled*): Social occasion? Who the devil said anything about social occasions?

DR. FELL: I thought *you* did. Please go on.

PENDLETON: It was a wet day in Kensal Green cemetery. There we were, a lot of middle-aged men, standing about an open grave in the rain. Feeling liverish; nothing right; you know how it is.

DR. FELL: Unfortunately, I do.

PENDLETON: I was arranging to get away next day for a long holiday in the south of France. After that I was giving up my house in St. John's Wood, and taking a flat closer to the West End. Light! Life! *Something!* I'd taken my secretary along to that infernal funeral in case I wanted to dictate any last letters. (*Suddenly struck by this*) Last letters! Never mind! (*Fade in sounds of rain*) As we were on our way out of the cemetery, we must have got confused, because . . . (*The voice fades into a long roll of thunder. The steady noise of rain backs the scene throughout.* PAMELA BENNETT *speaks. She is young and keeps her voice, as a rule, at a colourless level.*)

PAMELA: Mr. Pendleton, are you sure we haven't taken the wrong turning? This isn't the way to the car.

PENDLETON (*irritably*): You said it was, Miss Bennett.

PAMELA: No, sir. I said . . .

PENDLETON: Anyway, how can you expect to see anything in this rain? And all this nightmare of tombstones?

PAMELA: It looks like an older part of the cemetery.

PENDLETON: It is. It's where they bury you when you haven't much money. Always remember that, Miss Bennett.

PAMELA: I'm sorry if I got the directions mixed, Mr. Pendleton. I thought . . .

PENDLETON (*magnanimously*): Please don't mention it, Miss Bennett. It's a small matter, in fact, compared to other things. I'll pay you the compliment of saying you're the best secretary I ever had. Yet you want to leave me?

PAMELA: I want to get married, yes.

PENDLETON: That's what Mr. Fraser was telling me. (*Spitefully*) And who is this paragon of yours? What does he do? Does he make any money?

PAMELA: Frank's a radio technician. He's not very well-off, I admit.

PENDLETON: Well-off? I'll bet he doesn't make as much as I pay you, yet you want to get married!
(*Fade up rain.*)

PAMELA (*bewildered*): Is there anything so very strange about that?

PENDLETON: Yes, if it interferes with your career. It . . .
(*Peak and fade rain to background.*)

PAMELA (*as though alarmed*): What's wrong?

PENDLETON (*in a low voice*): Good . . . God!

PAMELA: What is it? Don't lower your umbrella like that, or you'll get soaking wet. What's wrong?

PENDLETON: Do you see that grave?

PAMELA: Which one?

PENDLETON: On the end. The very-much-neglected grave with the little stone cross. The name's almost effaced. Can you read it?

PAMELA (*slowly*): "Sacred to the Memory of Mary . . . Ellen . . . Kimball."

PENDLETON (*astonished*): So it is; so it is!

PAMELA: "Born . . ." No, I can't read that part of it. What about her?

PENDLETON (*genuinely moved*): Poor Mary Ellen! (*He sighs*) Now I come to think of it, she did have an aunt or someone living at Kensal Rise. It's a girl I used to know twenty-five, thirty years ago.

PAMELA: Did you know her well?

PENDLETON (*brooding*): I'll tell you a deep secret, Miss Bennett. I would have married her . . . yes, so help me! . . . only . . .

PAMELA: Only . . . what?

PENDLETON: Do I have to explain these things? I came from small beginnings. I had my way to make in the world. And she wouldn't have helped me.

PAMELA: I still don't think I understand.

PENDLETON (*dogmatically*): A man of my sort owes it to himself to make a wealthy marriage or none at all. That's what I've always said, and that's what I believe. Anything else is sentimental rubbish. I was sorry to break with her, but I thought it was kinder to break cleanly. I was sorry to hear of her death . . . that was years afterwards . . . (*Fade in thunder*) But . . . well, I had other things to think about.

PAMELA (*under her breath*): You *poisonous* . . . (*The word is almost but not quite drowned out by a roll of thunder.*)

PENDLETON (*startled, not hearing*): What's that? Did you say something?

PAMELA (*colourless again*): No, Mr. Pendleton. Hadn't we better get on to the car?

PENDLETON: Yes, I suppose so. (*Wistfully*) Poor Mary Ellen, though.

PAMELA: I'm sorry, Mr. Pendleton, but I've got suede shoes on, and this clay is ruining them. Couldn't we go on?

PENDLETON: She was a pretty little thing, and absolutely devoted to me. (*Defensively*) I was *sorry* for her, you know.

PAMELA: If you really feel like that, Mr. Pendleton . . .

PENDLETON: Well?

PAMELA: You could have her grave tidied up, and some flowers put on it. Shall I attend to it for you?

PENDLETON (*eagerly*): By George, yes! That's a good idea. She'd have liked that. But . . . how are they going to identify her?

PAMELA: Identify her?

PENDLETON: There must be thousands of graves here. Look!

PAMELA: Yes. Didn't you ever have anything to do with cemeteries, Mr. Pendleton?

PENDLETON (*shuddering*): No! I hate the thought of death! I . . .

PAMELA: Each grave has a number cut into the stone at one side. This one is Kensal Green 1-9-3-3.

PENDLETON (*blankly*): Kensal Green 1-9-3-3.

PAMELA: Sounds like a telephone number, doesn't it?

PENDLETON (*quietly*): Yes. Doesn't it? Kensal Green 1-9-3-3. Kensal Green 1-9-3-3.

PAMELA (*pleading*): *Couldn't* we go on now, Mr. Pendleton?

PENDLETON (*unheeding*): Make a note of that, Miss Bennett. Attend to it first thing next week, and . . . (*Waking up*) Wait a minute! I forgot. You're leaving the office. Has it ever occurred to you, Miss Bennett, that you take the most impossible times for inconveniencing me with your personal affairs?

PAMELA (*helplessly*): I'm sorry, Mr. Pendleton. I can't seem to do anything to please you today.

PENDLETON: You could please me, at least, by staying on at the office.

PAMELA: I've told you before that . . .

PENDLETON (*significantly*): You're not a bad-looking girl. I could do a lot for you, you know, if I wanted to.

PAMELA (*unemotionally*): As you did for Mary Ellen Kimball?

PENDLETON: Confound your impertinence!

PAMELA: Were *you* speaking of impertinence, Mr. Pendleton?

PENDLETON (*stiffly*): Perhaps you're right. Yes, I'm quite sure you're right. Shall we forget I ever mentioned it?

PAMELA: If you please.

PENDLETON (*blankly*): Kensal Green 1-9-3-3. Kensal Green 1-9-3-3.

PAMELA: Why do you keep on repeating that number?

PENDLETON: Not because I regret anything, mind you!

PAMELA: I'm sure you don't.

PENDLETON: After all, you can't take a girl like that into society. Not when she's thrown her cap over the windmill for you, and got herself talked about. It's just that her utter devotion touched me a good deal.

PAMELA: I'm sure it did.

PENDLETON: She always said she'd come back if I called her. And sometimes . . .

PAMELA: You felt like calling her?

PENDLETON: Years ago, maybe. But there she is with the worms and clay (*arrogantly*), and here *I* am where I've always wanted to be. It's too late now, isn't it?

PAMELA: Much too late, Mr. Pendleton. *Much too late.*

(*Swell thunder and then fade into* PENDLETON'S *voice.*)

PENDLETON: . . . and that, Dr. Fell, was all that happened at the cemetery. Little enough, you'd say. But it started preying on my mind. I couldn't forget that girl.

DR. FELL: You mean Miss Bennett?

PENDLETON (*impatiently*): Miss Bennett . . . No! I can't think what made me forget myself there. I mean Mary Ellen Kimball.

DR. FELL: You've made your mental state fairly clear, I think. And then?

PENDLETON: For some reason I began to get nervous. I lunched at my club, and couldn't eat. I went to my office, and couldn't work. That infernal number kept running through my head: Kensal Green 1-9-3-3. Then, when I went home in the evening . . . (*Abruptly*) Have you ever seen my house?

DR. FELL: I have not had that pleasure, sir. But I believe it's one of the showplaces of St. John's Wood.

PENDLETON (*bitterly*): Great ugly mausoleum of a place! I told you I was moving house, into a flat that'd suit me better when I came back from Europe. I knew most of the servants would be gone, of course. But I thought Mrs. Tancred—that's my housekeeper—would still be there. (*Fade in rain*) It was still raining, with thunder about. Then, when I went up the path about half-past six . . .

(*Swell rain and fade down. Distant ringing of a doorbell. A heavy door is opened.* MRS. TANCRED *is elderly and well-spoken.*)

MRS. TANCRED (*surprised*): Bless me, sir; I didn't know it was you.

(*Door shuts out the rain.*)

PENDLETON: Sorry to trouble you, Mrs. Tancred. I seem to have mislaid my latchkey. And yet I could have sworn I had it on my key-ring this morning.

MRS. TANCRED: It's no trouble, Mr. Pendleton.

PENDLETON (*irritably*): Confound it, what are all these packing-cases doing in the hall?

MRS. TANCRED (*reproachfully*): I hope you haven't forgotten you're leaving here, sir?

PENDLETON (*waking up*): Oh, yes. Yes, of course. Have you got my bags packed?

MRS. TANCRED: All ready for you, sir. Your hat and coat? Will you be dining at home tonight?

PENDLETON (*still rather dazed*): Yes. Yes, I suppose I'd better. For the last time.

MRS. TANCRED: It does seem a pity, doesn't it?

PENDLETON (*quickly*): What seems a pity?

MRS. TANCRED: Leaving here, after all these years.

PENDLETON (*hurriedly*): Now you've been a very good house-keeper, Mrs. Tancred. I've always treated *you* generously, haven't I? I've got you a good position to follow this one, haven't I?

MRS. TANCRED (*offended*): I wasn't meaning that, sir.

PENDLETON: Then what did you mean?

MRS. TANCRED: Breaking up a lovely home like this.

PENDLETON: *This?* This infernal picture gallery? Where I feel like . . . like old Scrooge every time I come home!

MRS. TANCRED (*sympathetically*): It must have been a bit lonely at times, I daresay.

PENDLETON (*fiercely*): Lonely? I am never lonely!

MRS. TANCRED (*submissively*): No, sir.

PENDLETON: There are a lot of people who envy me, Mrs. Tancred. And, what's more, I deserve their envy.

MRS. TANCRED: Yes, sir.

PENDLETON: I . . . (*giving it up*) . . . never mind. They haven't taken the furniture out of the library, have they?

MRS. TANCRED: No, sir. Only the books off the shelves.

PENDLETON: I shall be in the library, then. Dinner at seven-thirty. And . . . Mrs. Tancred!

MRS. TANCRED: Yes, sir?

PENDLETON: If I ever feel the need of any sympathy for my unhappy lot, I'll ask for it. Do I make myself quite clear?

MRS. TANCRED: Yes, sir. Just as you wish, sir.

(*Door opens and closes heavily. Slight pause.* PENDLETON *draws a deep breath.*)

PENDLETON (*muttering*): What's a library without books? Empty mortuary kind of place . . . Confound her; she's even taken the writing paper off my desk. Nothing's right. Nothing *has* ever been right! And where's my Venetian mirror? Have they gone and stolen my Ven . . . Oh, no. No. Here we are. (*Slight pause. He changes his tone.*) George Pendleton, my lad, you might as well face the fact that you can't stick dinner alone in this house tonight. Never mind *why* you can't do it. Never mind whether it's your health (*fade in rain*), or what it is. Rain going on forever. It'll be wet in that cemetery. And is there any reason on earth why you shouldn't go out for dinner and enjoy yourself? That's it! Ring Bill Fraser, and go out to dinner. Ring Bill Fraser. Telephone . . . here we are.

(*Noise of receiver lifted, and receiver-hook jiggled up and down.*)

PENDLETON: Hello! Hello! Hello!

OPERATOR: Number, please?

PENDLETON: Hello? I want . . . (*Groping*) Bill's number. Now what's Bill's number? What the devil *is* Bill's number?

OPERATOR: Number, please?

PENDLETON: I want . . . I want . . . (*Blurting it out*) Kensal Green 1-9-3-3. (*Heavy crash of thunder*) Good God! What have I said?

OPERATOR (*unemotionally*): Kensal Green 1-9-3-3.

PENDLETON (*in consternation*): Operator, wait! There's some mistake! I said the wrong thing! I want . . .

OPERATOR: Kensal Green 1-9-3-3.

(*Ringing tone. Then a woman's voice answers; it is a girlish voice, very faint and almost whispering.*)

VOICE: Yes? Who is it?

PENDLETON (*wildly*): There's been some mist . . .

VOICE (*with sudden eagerness*): George dear, is that you?

PENDLETON (*alarmed*): Who is that? Who's speaking?

VOICE: It's Mary Ellen, dear. Don't you recognize my voice?

PENDLETON: No! No! No!

VOICE: I knew you'd call me sooner or later, dear. But I've waited *ever* so long.

PENDLETON: I . . .

VOICE (*eagerly*): And of course I'll come if you want me. I'll be there just as soon as I can.

PENDLETON: I tell you—!

VOICE: I'll be there by seven o'clock, truly I will. But you mustn't be frightened at how I look now.

PENDLETON: You're not Mary Ellen! This is a trick! *Mary Ellen is dead!*

VOICE: Yes, dear. But the dead sleep lightly. And they can be lonely too.

PENDLETON: Don't talk to me! You can't talk to me! I won't listen to you! I . . .

VOICE: I'll wear a veil, dear. Because I'm not very pretty now. But I won't hurt you, my darling. Truly I won't!

PENDLETON (*frantically*): Go away, do you hear? Go . . .

VOICE: Goodbye, dear. Remember, when the clock strikes seven. (*There is a click and a long pause.*)

PENDLETON (*breathing hard*): Mrs. Tancred! (*Shouting*) Mrs. Tancred!

(*Door opens.*)

MRS. TANCRED (*flustered*): Lord 'a' mercy, sir, what's the matter? (*Door shuts.*)

PENDLETON (*levelly but hoarsely*): Who's been playing tricks on me?

MRS. TANCRED: Tricks, sir?

PENDLETON: I want to know who's been playing the fool with this telephone.

MRS. TANCRED (*surprised*): Nobody, sir. It's only what you ordered. (*Nervously amused*) You haven't been trying to *use* the phone, have you?

PENDLETON: Use it? I rang up a friend of mine. A woman's voice answered and pretended to be somebody I used to know years ago . . .

MRS. TANCRED (*alarmed and offended*): Now, sir, stop your joking.

PENDLETON: You think I'm *joking?*

MRS. TANCRED (*commiseratingly*): You're all upset, that's what it is. Sit down by the desk. Hang up the receiver and put the phone down. . . . There!

PENDLETON (*desperately*): Will you kindly tell me . . . ?

MRS. TANCRED: You didn't use that telephone, sir. Nobody could have used that phone.

PENDLETON: And why not?

MRS. TANCRED: Because it was disconnected this morning. (*After a pause, she continues patiently.*) You're giving up the house, sir. Don't you remember? You ordered the telephone to be removed. The man came this morning, and disconnected all the wires, and took the metal box off the baseboard of the wall.

PENDLETON (*not loudly*): Are you mad, or am I?

MRS. TANCRED: Just look for yourself, then. There's the flex of the phone hanging halfway down to the floor. It ends in midair; it's not connected with anything.

PENDLETON (*breathing it*): That's . . . true!

MRS. TANCRED: Of course it's true.

PENDLETON: The phone's *not* connected. It wasn't connected when I spoke to . . .

MRS. TANCRED: When I saw you there with the phone in your hand, and the receiver off the hook, and the cord not going anywhere, and looking as though you'd really *been* talking to somebody . . . (*Doubtfully*) You *were* just pretending, weren't you, sir?

PENDLETON: What if I said no?

MRS. TANCRED: Really, Mr. Pendleton! Please!

PENDLETON: I tell you, I was talking to a woman on this telephone just before you came in here!

MRS. TANCRED (*flatly*): Indeed, sir.

PENDLETON: You don't believe me, do you?

MRS. TANCRED: I must ask to be excused, if you don't mind. I'm the only person here, and I've got to see to your dinner, and . . .

(*Door opens.*)

PENDLETON (*hoarsely*): Mrs. Tancred! Wait a minute!

MRS. TANCRED: Yes, sir?

PENDLETON: Mrs. Tancred (*pause*), how long have you been my housekeeper?

MRS. TANCRED: Three years and eight months. Why, sir?

PENDLETON: Sometimes, in certain lights, I get the notion we'd met before you came here.

MRS. TANCRED: Indeed, sir.

PENDLETON (*sharply*): Had we met before?

MRS. TANCRED: If I'd ever met you, sir, it isn't likely I should have forgotten you. Now is it?

PENDLETON: Mrs. Tancred! Wait! Don't go away! You're not going to leave me here alone?

MRS. TANCRED: Leave you alone? A big, able-bodied man! Really, sir!

(*Door closes.*)

PENDLETON: Mrs. Tancred! (*Desperately*) Mrs. Tancred! What . . . time is it?

MRS. TANCRED (*coldly, through closed door*): There's a clock on the mantel in there, sir. It must be . . .

(*Clock slowly strikes seven. Music up.*)

DR. FELL: I see, Mr. Pendleton. I see. But surely the story doesn't end there?

PENDLETON (*huskily*): End there . . . how do you mean?

DR. FELL: The clock strikes. The mystic hour arrives. Well? Did the ghostly visitor appear?

PENDLETON: I don't know.

DR. FELL: You don't know?

PENDLETON: I lost my head and bolted out of that house as though the devil were after me. Maybe he was.

DR. FELL: And afterwards?

PENDLETON: I spent the night at a hotel. Going abroad today was out of the question. I'm a practical man; I had to *know.*

DR. FELL: You . . . investigated?

PENDLETON: I got in touch with the telephone people. That phone was disconnected yesterday morning. Besides, I could see that for myself. I can take my living oath there was no wire leading from that phone.

DR. FELL: Yet you heard a voice speaking from the receiver?

PENDLETON: I did.

DR. FELL: Mary Ellen Kimball's voice?

PENDLETON (*after a pause*): Yes.

DR. FELL: I see. Did you find out anything else in your investigations today?

PENDLETON: There's no doubt she's dead, if that's what you mean. I couldn't find her aunt at Kensal Rise . . . the aunt's gone away as a servant or something. But I found the doctor who attended Mary Ellen. She died of pneumonia brought on by . . . (*Hesitates*)

DR. FELL: Brought on by what?

PENDLETON: Well. Brought on by undernourishment. Anyway, she died. Called herself Mrs. Kimball.

DR. FELL (*quickly*): Why did she call herself Mrs. Kimball?

PENDLETON (*just as quickly*): I don't know.

DR. FELL: I must repeat the question, my good sir. It may be the most important thing in the whole affair. Why did she call herself Mrs. Kimball?

PENDLETON: I tell you, I don't know!

DR. FELL (*persuasively*): Mr. Pendleton, I am at the service of anyone with a problem in his head or a trouble on his back. But if you won't tell me the truth about this . . .

PENDLETON: You mean you won't help me?

DR. FELL: How can I?

PENDLETON: Look here, Dr. Fell. I've been through a lot already. I don't propose to be questioned and cross-questioned about something I don't think is important.

DR. FELL: Why not let *me* be the judge of that?

PENDLETON: If you think I'm afraid to go back to that house to-night, you're mistaken. (*Blustering*) I'm not without people I pay, and pay well, to look after me. There's Wilmot, for one.

DR. FELL (*sharply*): Wilmot? Who's Wilmot?

PENDLETON: My chauffeur. He's outside in the car now.

DR. FELL: Is Wilmot by any chance a young man?

PENDLETON: Yes, fairly young. Very (*mockingly*) superior sort of chap, but reliable. Why?

DR. FELL: It may not mean anything. It probably doesn't.

PENDLETON: As a matter of fact, I'd already had a word about this with a friend of mine at Scotland Yard. Superintendent Hadley.

DR. FELL: Oh? You've mentioned this to Hadley?

PENDLETON: Unofficially, of course.

DR. FELL: And what did *he* say?

PENDLETON: He told me to see you. I came here, fair and square, to get advice. And do I get advice? No! I get a lot of wrangling and quibbling when I'm trying to tell my story. I can't go to the police; I can't go to you; where *can* I go?

DR. FELL: If I were less polite, sir, I should tell you.

PENDLETON: That's your last word?

DR. FELL: Until you say yours.

PENDLETON (*grimly*): All right! I'll take it as that. Where's that manservant of yours? (*Calling*) Hoy!
(*Door opens.*)

HOSKINS: Yes, sir?

PENDLETON: Get me my hat and coat, please.

HOSKINS: Got 'em right 'ere, sir. (*Conversationally*) Wind's rising tonight, gentlemen.

DR. FELL: Blowing hard, is it?

HOSKINS: Regular gale, and black as your hat.

PENDLETON (*bursting out*): And you want me to go home alone?

DR. FELL: Look here, man; why not be sensible? Tell me the whole story.

PENDLETON: I've told just as much as I'm going to tell this side of eternity. If anything happens to me, it's on your own head. Good night, and I can find my own way out.

DR. FELL (*under his breath*): Hoskins!

HOSKINS: Yes, sir?

DR. FELL (*in a low voice*): When you've seen Mr. Pendleton out, bring my cloak and walking-stick. . . .

HOSKINS: Stop a bit, sir! You're not . . .

DR. FELL: Quiet! He's on the stairs; he'll hear you. Close the door.

HOSKINS: Yes, sir.

(*Door closes.*)

DR. FELL (*querulously*): Now he's made me feel like a selfish hound. I suppose I've got to follow him.

HOSKINS: You're not going out of the house tonight, sir?

DR. FELL (*with dignity*): And why not, my good custodian?

HOSKINS: 'Cos you oughtn't to be out at any time, that's why. You haven't got the foggiest idea where you're going; you concentrate across the street against a red light; you walk off Underground platforms onto trains that ain't there . . .

DR. FELL (*with still more dignity*): If you are implying, my good Hoskins, that I occasionally suffer from a slight . . . a very slight . . . absent-mindedness . . .

HOSKINS (*awed*): Absent-mindedness, sir?

DR. FELL: That was the word.

HOSKINS: So help me, sir, when you was solving that Vickerly case, you came home cold sober and stood for twenty minutes trying to open the front door with a corkscrew.

DR. FELL: Listen to me, Hoskins.

HOSKINS: Yes, sir?

DR. FELL: Our friend Pendleton is going to have a bad night. Probably the worst night of his life. He may be in real danger.

HOSKINS: If you've got to go out, sir, let me ring Superintendent Hadley and have him meet you.

DR. FELL: Oh, no, my lad. No. We don't want the police in this.

HOSKINS: The man's in danger, but you *don't* want the police?

DR. FELL: That's exactly what I mean. Wait till he's gone, and then get me a taxi. What is he going to see in that house tonight? *What* is he going to see in that house tonight?

(Music up and down. Sounds of wind and a motorcar, which approaches and stops.)

TAXI DRIVER: I'm sorry about the engine trouble, governor. But I couldn't make it any sooner.

(Car door opens. Grunt suggesting heavy body getting out. Door closes.)

DR. FELL *(grimly resigned)*: That's all right. It can't be helped. You're sure this is where Mr. Pendleton lives?

DRIVER: Dead sure, governor. You can't mistake those funny towers and the fir trees growing up the path. *(Breaking off)* Hullo! There's somebody standing by the gate.

DR. FELL *(calling sharply)*: Who's there? Who's there?

(SUPERINTENDENT HADLEY has a military voice and a no-nonsense manner.)

HADLEY: *I'm* here, Fell. And wishing to blazes I'd stayed at the pub.

DR. FELL: That's not Hadley? Superintendent Hadley?

HADLEY: Oh, yes, it is. Waiting for twenty minutes in the perishing cold, while . . .

DR. FELL: But how did *you* get here?

HADLEY *(surprised)*: You sent for me, didn't you?

DR. FELL: *I* sent for you?

HADLEY: Hoskins did, anyway. He said it was an urgent matter for the police. He said . . .

DR. FELL: So the blighter's disobeyed my orders again. *(Breaking off)* That's all, driver. Good night.

DRIVER: Good night, governor.

(Taxi moves away.)

HADLEY: Let me get things straight, Fell. This is George Pendleton's house. I was here two years ago about a little matter of a burglary, and I know. You didn't drag me here at this hour to discuss that crazy yarn about a dead woman and a ghost telephone?

DR. FELL *(rather testily)*: My good Hadley, I didn't drag you here to discuss anything. I gather, though, you didn't believe the yarn?

HADLEY (*past comment*): Believe it? For the love of . . . !

DR. FELL: There's no time to argue that. The point is, did Pendleton get home safely tonight?

HADLEY: *I* don't know. There's a light in the library, anyway. (*Wind up*) Look up the path, past the fir trees. Those two French windows to the left of the front door.

DR. FELL: And one of these French windows, you notice, is standing part-way open.

HADLEY: Well? What about it?

DR. FELL: It's a fine night for that, isn't it?

HADLEY (*impatiently*): Maybe it blew open. Maybe Pendleton likes fresh air. Maybe . . .

(PAMELA's *voice cries out as though startled.*)

HADLEY: I *beg* your pardon, miss. It's so dark here I didn't see you.

PAMELA (*tense but composed*): That's quite all right. But would you mind letting me through the gate, please?

DR. FELL: Do you by any chance want to go in and see Mr. Pendleton?

PAMELA (*surprised*): Yes, of course. I . . . why do you ask that?

DR. FELL: I ask because my friend here is Superintendent Hadley from Scotland Yard . . .

PAMELA (*startled*): Scotland Yard?

DR. FELL: And I am Dr. Gideon Fell, an old scatter-brain occasionally found where there's trouble.

PAMELA: I'm Pamela Bennett. Mr. Pendleton's secretary. I came here because of Mrs. Tancred. She phoned the office today. She said Mr. Pendleton had gone rushing out last night, leaving his suitcases and everything else in the house, and hadn't been back since. He hasn't been in touch with the office, either. Mr. Fraser was worried. He asked me if I'd come round here, and . . . Mr. Pendleton *is* all right, isn't he?

DR. FELL: I very much fear he isn't.

HADLEY: Don't talk nonsense, Fell!

DR. FELL: It may *be* nonsense, of course. I've talked a lot of it in my time. But let's go in and see him, Hadley. Let's face the powers of darkness in their lair. Let's open the gate . . .

(*Metallic creaking of the gate. Then* WILMOT *speaks: a soft, insinuating, well-bred voice. He is in his middle twenties and speaks as one trying to be agreeable.*)

WILMOT: If I were you, gentlemen, *I* shouldn't touch that gate.

PAMELA (*crying out*): Who spoke then? (*No reply, except the whistling of the wind*) I heard somebody! Who was it?

WILMOT: You heard *me,* young lady. I'm inside the gate; you're outside. Let's leave it at that.

HADLEY (*exasperated*): Look here, young fellow, what's going on in this place? Who *are* you?

WILMOT: My name is Wilmot. I turn an electric torch round and . . . notice my chauffeur's uniform. Also notice the rifle in my other hand.

HADLEY: I'm a police officer, cocky. What's the idea of the rifle?

WILMOT: The governor's orders are to patrol these grounds and make sure nobody gets in. I'm doing it.

HADLEY: And has anybody got in?

WILMOT: No. Not a living soul.

DR. FELL: That's an interesting choice of phrase, young man. If you're Mr. Pendleton's chauffeur . . .

WILMOT: Such is my humble position, Dr. Fell.

DR. FELL (*sharply*): You know who I am?

WILMOT: As a matter of fact, I just recognized you. I drove the boss to your house tonight. *Is* this man here a police officer?

DR. FELL: Yes. And the young lady beside me is Mr. Pendleton's secretary.

WILMOT: Excuse me if I didn't recognize her. I haven't been on this job very long.

PAMELA: Mr. Pendleton *is* all right, isn't he?

WILMOT: He couldn't be in a happier state. I drove him to Dr. Fell's; I brought him back safely; I delivered him to the mercies of Mrs. Tancred; I went down the street to put the car away . . .

DR. FELL: If you went to put the car away, how can you be sure nobody's got in?

WILMOT (*sharply*): It's impossible!

DR. FELL: Why?

WILMOT: That was half an hour ago!

DR. FELL: He could have died half an hour ago.

PAMELA: Don't *say* that!

WILMOT (*quickly*): His Nibs was upset about something; I'll give you that. He went lurching up the path talking to himself, and Mrs. Tancred couldn't do anything with him.

DR. FELL: What was he talking to himself about?

WILMOT: *I* don't know. Some woman or other. He said he was going to ring her up and dare her to come back again.

DR. FELL (*quietly*): Look here, Hadley. We've *got* to go up there now.

HADLEY: But what in blazes do you think is wrong? He couldn't have been attacked without an outcry. And there hasn't been a sound. Look at this place. Only that little light from the library. Dark, silent, and peaceful as the gra— (*A woman's distant scream, very shrill*) What was that?

PAMELA: It sounded like a woman's voice!

DR. FELL (*grimly*): Would anybody like to bet it isn't Mrs. Tancred?

PAMELA: Look! It *is* Mrs. Tancred! She's coming out of that open French window, and she looks . . .

MRS. TANCRED (*calling*): Wilmot! Wilmot! Wilmot!

WILMOT (*calling*): I'm here, Mrs. Tancred! Out by the gate!
(MRS. TANCRED *is almost hysterically frightened, but trying to be steady.*)

MRS. TANCRED: He said he didn't want any sympathy. All right! He won't *get* any sympathy. Just as though a body didn't try to do the best she could every single day of her life, and . . . and . . . for God's sake, get a doctor!

WILMOT: You don't mean it's the governor?

MRS. TANCRED: "If ever I need any sympathy for my unhappy lot" . . . that's just what he said . . . "I'll ask for it." All right! Let him try to ask for it *now*, and see if anybody cares!

HADLEY: What is it, ma'am? What's wrong?

MRS. TANCRED: It's murder, that's what it is! He's lying on the floor in the library with the telephone beside him. His face is an awful colour, and I don't think he's breathing.

WILMOT: There hasn't been a sound out of that house. I swear there hasn't!

MRS. TANCRED: No, of course there wasn't a sound. All I did was go in and ask him if he wanted some coffee. And there he was in a dim little ugly light, with his face as blue as though he'd had a stroke. . . .

HADLEY: As though he'd had a stroke, eh? Then what's all this about murder?

MRS. TANCRED: I tell you, his face . . . ! And then there's the clay tracked across the floor, from the window to where he's lying. There's even wet clay on Mr. Pendleton, as though . . .

HADLEY: As though . . . what?

MRS. TANCRED (*slowly*): As though somebody covered with clay had tried to hold him.

(*Music up and down. A door opens.*)

DR. FELL (*musing*): And this, apparently, is the famous library. This is the place where bogies walk and a telephone talks of its own accord.

PAMELA (*urgently*): Dr. Fell! Please!

DR. FELL: "From the hag and the hungry goblin
      That into rags would rend ye:
    And the spirit that stands by the evil lands
      In the book of moons . . . defend ye!"
(*Waking up*) Er . . . I beg your pardon. What's that?

PAMELA: Dr. Fell, you've got to tell me. Is he . . . dead?

DR. FELL: No, Miss Bennett. He's not dead. Hadley and Wilmot have carried him upstairs. He's had a bad heart attack. But I'm afraid he'll pull through.

PAMELA (*surprised*): You're *afraid* he'll pull through?

DR. FELL: If Mr. George Pendleton has got a soul, it must be a pretty shabby one. (*Casually*) Don't you think so?

PAMELA (*hesitating*): I didn't exactly like him, no. But you get *used* to a person, I suppose. I shouldn't like to think he was . . .

DR. FELL: Haunted to death?

(*Gust of wind rises strongly. Wooden noise suggesting flapping of window.*)

DR. FELL: Don't be frightened, Miss Bennett. It's only the French window banging.

PAMELA: I'm not frightened. At least . . . not much. What did you mean by "haunted to death"?

DR. FELL (*unheeding*): There's the claw-footed desk. There's the Venetian mirror where his own reflection scared him. There's the famous telephone. There's the line of clay marks. There's the whole show-piece of death and terror, my dear.

PAMELA (*more loudly*): What did you mean by "haunted to death"?

DR. FELL: Just that, my dear. Literally that.

PAMELA: You mean he's been haunted by—by a dead person?

DR. FELL: Oh, no. Not at all. I mean he's been haunted by a very much living person.

PAMELA: Dr. Fell!

DR. FELL (*musingly*): What's your opinion of Mrs. Tancred, by the way? With her demure grey hair and her great devotion?

PAMELA: What on earth has Mrs. Tancred got to do with this? Or Wilmot or anybody here?

DR. FELL (*with lordly effect*): "I can call spirits from the vasty deep." "Ay, but will they come, if you do call them?" (*Changing his tone, distressed*) Especially by telephone. Oh, my eye! Surely it's plain that some person . . . one single person . . . has been trying to scare that man out of his wits? Don't you see now what happened here tonight?

PAMELA: No, I don't think I do.

DR. FELL: As Pendleton sat here in the dim little ugly light, a ghostly figure appeared at that French window. It wore long old-fashioned skirts and heavy black veil. It walked towards him, tracking graveyard clay. It stretched out its arms to him, like this . . .

PAMELA: Dr. Fell, please keep away from me! You look . . .

DR. FELL: Forgive me. I was (*clearing his throat*) carried away. (*Pause*) Would you care to hear how the whole trick was worked?

PAMELA: Trick! What trick?

DR. FELL: Has anyone told you about the ghost-voice on the disconnected telephone?

PAMELA: Yes, Mrs. Tancred was gabbling something about it. But . . .

DR. FELL: Suppose you ask, as Pendleton did, to have a telephone disconnected. They disconnect it at the Central Exchange. If you're leaving the house, they come round and collect it later. But, my dear Miss Bennett, I'll tell you what they *don't* do.

PAMELA: Well?

DR. FELL: They don't send a man round to yank the whole apparatus off the wall, put it on the desk, and say he'll be back for it next day. That's obvious nonsense.

PAMELA: You mean Mrs. Tancred wasn't telling the truth when she said that?

DR. FELL: Oh, no. She was telling the truth. But this "man from the telephone company" was an imposter.

PAMELA: The man from the telephone company . . . who was he?

DR. FELL: Can't you guess?

PAMELA: No, I don't think so. What did he do?

DR. FELL: He took away the real phone and substituted a "spirit telephone." You don't know what a "spirit telephone" is?

PAMELA: No, of course not.

DR. FELL: It's an old device used by fake spiritualists. You see a telephone, without wires, standing on a desk. Like that one on the floor now. You lift the receiver and talk to the dead. Of course, you never really talk into the phone at all.

PAMELA: But if you don't really talk into the phone, then how . . . ?

DR. FELL: Fixed underneath the desk is a tiny two-button microphone, with hidden wires leading to another room in the same house. The microphone under the desk picks up every word you think you're saying to that telephone. Am I clear?

PAMELA: Yes, I think so.

DR. FELL: The dummy telephone contains a low-power radio receiving unit. Somebody in another room can talk back to you, with every possible ghostly effect . . . Would you mind picking up the telephone now?

PAMELA: You don't mean it works now?

DR. FELL: Oh, no. It's been changed. Just pick it up.

PAMELA: All right. There you are.

DR. FELL: If Pendleton hadn't rung Kensal Green 1-9-3-3, then rest assured that same number would have rung *him*.

PAMELA: The scheme couldn't fail either way?

DR. FELL: Correct.

PAMELA (*tensely*): The ghost-voice, you said, came from a room in this house?

DR. FELL: Yes. I can't tell you which one, because the mechanism's been removed.

PAMELA: Then the person responsible for it must *live* in this house.

DR. FELL: Not necessarily. You see, there's one thing I guess . . . I firmly believe . . . but I can't prove.

PAMELA: Oh? And what's that?

DR. FELL: Tell me, Miss Bennett, just *why* did you work this whole trick? Why did you try to scare your father to death? (*Crash of an object dropped on the floor;* DR. FELL *continues mildly.*) Don't drop the telephone, my dear. Pendleton surely *is* your father, isn't he? And the late Mary Ellen Kimball was your mother?

PAMELA (*through her teeth*): I do not like you, Doctor Fell. The reason why I cannot tell . . .

DR. FELL (*heartily*): Now I, on the other hand, admire you tremendously. (*Deprecating*) But my dear girl, hang it all, I knew you must be behind this when I heard your fiancé is a radio technician.

PAMELA: You leave Frank out of this!

DR. FELL: This fiancé, I imagine, installed the ghost-mechanism and took it away today. He probably thought it was only a joke.

PAMELA: He did! I swear he did!

DR. FELL: There was surely a reason, you see, why Mary Ellen Kimball called herself Mrs. Kimball. *You* led Pendleton to the wrong gate in the cemetery, past that neglected grave. *You* put it into his mind. *You* suggested the telephone number. *You* stole his latchkey to this house, since he had it at the office that morning. You needed that key to come and go as you liked, and impersonate the two voices on the phone. Then when you were ready for your last appearance tonight . . .

PAMELA (*fiercely*): Is there any need to go on with this? He killed her.

DR. FELL (*startled*): You mean Pendleton killed your mother?

PAMELA: Oh, not cleanly. Not with a knife or a bullet or poison. All he did was break her heart and leave her to starve.

DR. FELL: Did he know about you?

PAMELA: He knew there *was* a child; that's all.

DR. FELL: Yes, I thought he knew it.

PAMELA: But she was too proud to ask for anything. And he (*mimicking*) "had other things to think about." I think I've dreamed all my life of getting close to him, one day, when he didn't know who I was.

DR. FELL: For the love of Mike, go easy! If somebody should come in here now . . .

PAMELA: I've done what I wanted to do. I've torn his whole rotten life in pieces; and there he is gasping for breath up-

stairs; and I'm glad! I'm . . . (*Breaking down*) Oh, God, I
can't go on with this! Call your superintendent and give the
game away. *I'm* not sorry!

DR. FELL (*amazed*): Just one moment. Hey! You don't think *I'm*
going to tell Hadley anything?

PAMELA (*taken aback*): Aren't you? Isn't that why you're here?

DR. FELL: On the contrary, I've been trying to keep the police
away from this house all evening.

PAMELA: What's the good of trying to hide it, even if I wanted
to? *They'll* find out!

DR. FELL: Are you quite sure they'll find out?

PAMELA: Look at the clay marks on the floor.

DR. FELL: Those footprints can't be identified, you know.
They're only smudges.

PAMELA: I think I can hear somebody outside in the hall. If it's
Superintendent Hadley . . .

DR. FELL (*grimly*): If it is, my dear, and you dare to say one
word about this . . .

PAMELA: Then who made the footprints?

DR. FELL (*blandly*): Didn't you know? Why, Pendleton made
them himself.

PAMELA: What on earth are you talking about?

DR. FELL: Hadley thinks the esteemed gentleman is mad. Obviously, of course, he is mad. He kept dashing to that window
on the lookout for a pursuing ghost. So he tracked in clay
soil from the garden, and collapsed here when he heard an
imaginary noise.

PAMELA: But his shoes! There'll be no clay on his shoes!

DR. FELL: Oh, yes, there will. Please remember that the gentleman didn't come home last night or take a suitcase with
him. His shoes, if I'm not mistaken, will still bear excellent
traces of the clay he really did get yesterday in Kensal
Green cemetery. (*Complacently*) I often think that I should
have made an admirable criminal myself.

HADLEY (*from a distance*): Dr. Fell! Dr. Fell! Where are you?

DR. FELL (*galvanized*): There's Hadley now! If you don't keep
your head and brace up, I'll come and haunt you myself.
Don't turn on the tears now, when you've come through all
the rest of it with a poker face. Just keep repeating after me,
"I do not like you, Doctor Fell . . ."

(*Door opens.*)

HADLEY: Look here, my fat detective; there's been no crime committed in this place. Pendleton's own shoes . . .

DR. FELL (*loudly*): Oh, Miss Bennett, what were you saying?

PAMELA (*hysterically*): Nothing! Nothing at . . .

DR. FELL (*reciting, still more loudly*): I do not like you, Doctor Fell, the reason why I cannot tell . . .

PAMELA (*almost crying*): But this I know, and know full well . . . I think *I like you,* Dr. Fell!

(*Music up.*)

August 28, 1943.

Carr rarely transferred his novels or short stories bodily to the radio. In the few instances that he did so, he chose stories that are particularly suited to a listening audience. "Death Has Four Faces" is a re-telling of his too-little-known story "The Silver Curtain." The clicking of the ball in the roulette wheel and the beating of the rain as the murder is committed are compellingly effective on the radio.

We are all gamblers one way or another. But what kind of odds did Ralph Harvey accept? *Faites vos jeux.*

Death Has Four Faces

THE CHARACTERS:

Jean Goron	Prefect of Police
Mary Stanhope	Who watches the gamblers
Ralph Harvey	Who loses at roulette
Ferdie Davos	Who pays for medicine
Dr. Lasalle	Who dispenses medicine
Mercier	Agent de Police
Croupier	

Setting: La Bandelette, France, 1930s.

NARRATOR: Tonight's story, I confess, intrigues me; it is another instance from my notebook of the miracle which turns out to be no miracle. You are warned, good friends, that I shall try to deceive you until the end. The town of La Bandelette on the northeast coast of France. (*Slight pause*) Don't we remember, with more than a little nostalgia, La Bandelette before the war? Its gabled and queerly painted houses like a town in a Disney film? Its pine-scented air? Its open carriages that clopped and jingled along its broad avenues? Its two great hotels, the Donjon and the Picardy, gay with coloured awnings and piling sham Gothic turrets into the sky? And at night, while the lighthouse beam revolved, its casino —a paradise of English gamblers for baccarat, for chemin-de-fer, and for roulette?

CROUPIER: *Faites vos jeux, messieurs et mesdames! Faites vos jeux!*

NARRATOR: And the ivory ball flicking in the glittering wheel? And the long board with its red and black numbers? And the croupier's eternal song?

CROUPIER: *Les jeux sont faits! Rien ne va plus!*

NARRATOR: Now it happened one night that there walked in the red, soft-carpeted gaming rooms Monsieur Jean Goron, the Prefect of Police. A round, amiable, catlike man, with a white rose in his buttonhole; a small king in La Bandelette. He beamed still more with pride because he was escorting a remarkably attractive English girl. And, as they stood on the edge of the crowd at the largest roulette table . . .

(*Crowd murmurs.*)

GORON: Well, mademoiselle? Do you enjoy it?

(MARY STANHOPE *is in her middle twenties. Sympathetic without being too naive.*)

MARY: I love it, Monsieur Goron!

GORON (*complacently*): I have promised your father you shall see La Bandelette. *Enfin,* you shall *see* La Bandelette.

CROUPIER: *Faites vos jeux, messieurs et mesdames! Faites vos jeux!*

MARY: Monsieur Goron.

GORON: Yes, mademoiselle?

MARY: The croupier's spun the wheel. He's even thrown the ball into it. But people are still putting counters on the table. Is that allowed?

GORON: But yes, my dear. They may place those bets until the wheel shall begin—what you call—slow down. Yes. Then the croupier will say . . .

CROUPIER: *Les jeux sont faits! Rien ne va plus! Rien ne va plus!* (*The murmur of voices dies abruptly to dead silence. We hear the ball clicking in the wheel.*)

MARY (*under her breath*): Look! How quiet they all are!

GORON (*under his breath*): They are praying, mademoiselle.

CROUPIER (*slowly*): *Nu-mé-ro . . . numéro vingt-quatre! Noir, pair, et passe!*

(*The murmur—half pleased, half angry—bursts out.*)

GORON: Number twenty-four.

MARY: What else did he say?

GORON (*lyrically*): Black, even, and above eighteen. And the rake goes out to sweep in the counters. And some are pleased, and some are sick; and all is music to a gambler's ear.

MARY (*abruptly*): He's lost again! *He's* looking sick!

GORON (*startled*): Pardon, mademoiselle?

MARY (*under her breath*): That light-haired young man, rather nice-looking, on the other side of the table.

GORON: What about him?

MARY: He's been steadily backing thirteen with the maximum stake, and—

GORON (*apprehensively*): This young man. You are—ah—interested in him?

MARY (*surprised*): Good heavens, no!

CROUPIER: *Faites vos jeux, messieurs et mesdames! Faites vos jeux!*

MARY: There he goes again! Not even a *carré* or a *transversale.* Thirteen to win. If he loses those last counters—

GORON: Mademoiselle is sure there is no—ah—?

MARY: But—I don't even know anything about him except his name. Ralph Harvey. We're staying at the same hotel. We've said hello in the lift, that's all.

GORON (*weightily*): In my experience of France, mademoiselle, saying hello leads to saying other things as well. And I have promised your father . . .

CROUPIER: *Faites vos jeux! Faites vos jeux! Faites vos jeux!*

MARY: He's lighting a cigarette as though it didn't matter. But I'll bet it *does* matter.

GORON (*distressed*): Mademoiselle! It is nothing! I assure you!

MARY: Why do you say that?

GORON: Because I am Prefect of Police.

MARY: Well?

GORON: I know these young English. Each year they come here, and they lose what you call the shirt. There will, perhaps, be trouble about his hotel bill. But—

(*Again the murmur stops to dead silence while we hear the wheel clicking.*)

GORON (*nervously muttering*): After all, one imagines, number thirteen must win *some* time.

MARY: I hope it does! I hope it does!

CROUPIER: *Nu-mé-ro . . .*

MARY (*whispering*): Come on, thirteen! Come on, thirteen! Come on, th—

CROUPIER: *Numéro sept! Rouge, impair, et manquel*

(*Murmur starts to rise.*)

MARY: That's done it. He's leaving the table.

GORON (*with authority*): Mademoiselle! If you please! Come with me!

MARY: Where?

GORON: A little way back from the crowd, please. Because I wish to speak seriously with you. (*Crowd murmur fades;* GORON *continues urgently.*) You are Miss Mary Stanhope, the daughter of my old friend. And you must not be stupid! If you think this Mr.—Mr. Harvey is apt to go into the garden and shoot himself . . .

MARY: He might do just that, you know!

GORON: Observe, mademoiselle, that he still has money.

MARY: How should I observe that?

GORON: Because he is headed straight for the bar. Look! The glass doors with "American Bar" above them. And— (*Stops short*)

MARY (*quickly*): What is it?

GORON (*tone changing sharply*): Ah, no! No! This is different. This I don't like at all!

MARY: What *is* it? What's wrong?

GORON: Do you notice who is following your friend into the bar? The short, thickset young man with the flat nose?

MARY: Well? What about him?

GORON: He is a crook, mademoiselle.

MARY: A crook? Who is he?

GORON: His name is Davos. He is half English and half heaven knows what. When he has a crooked game on hand—and God knows that is often—always he whistles the same tune. (GORON *whistles a few notes of "Auprès de ma Blonde" and breaks off impatiently.*) Never mind, never mind! But that robbery at the Hotel Donjon . . .

MARY: Robbery?

GORON: Davos sees that your friend is losing heavily. Davos follows him into the bar. I would give much, I assure you, to hear their conversation.

(*Brief musical bridge.* RALPH HARVEY *is a pleasant type, late twenties; not stricken in the way* MARY *thinks, but depressed and on edge.*)

RALPH: Barman.

BARMAN: Yes, Monsieur Harvey?

RALPH: Whisky and soda, please.

BARMAN (*cheerfully*): One *visky-soda.* Yes, monsieur.

(*Off,* DAVOS *whistles "Auprès de ma Blonde," breaking off in the middle.* DAVOS *is about thirty, well-spoken and com-*

pletely without foreign accent. He has a fat, bored, offhanded voice never far from a slight sneer.)

DAVOS: Barman, make that two.

BARMAN: Two *visky-soda.* Yes, Monsieur Davos.

DAVOS: Bar's completely deserted at this time of the night. Mind if I sit on the stool beside you?

RALPH: No. Not at all.

DAVOS: Thank you. I . . . eh . . . cigarette?

RALPH (*slight hesitation*): Thanks.

DAVOS: Light?

RALPH: Thanks.

DAVOS: I'm Ferdie Davos, by the way. Everybody knows me.

RALPH: My name's Ralph Harvey.

(*Two splashes from soda siphon. Glasses are slid on counter.*)

BARMAN: *Voila, messieurs! Deux visky-soda.*

DAVOS: No, no, old man! No. The drinks are on me. We can't let you spend your last fifty-franc note, now can we?

RALPH (*puzzled*): But look here—!

DAVOS: Here you are, barman. Keep the change.

BARMAN: *Mer-ci, monsieur!*

DAVOS (*complacently*): Now you had bad luck tonight, old man. *I* didn't. Notecase: see? Stuffed to bursting!

RALPH: I envy you.

DAVOS: What made you back number thirteen?

RALPH: Oh, I don't know. Cussedness, maybe. I've always felt like that.

DAVOS: Broke, eh?

RALPH (*lightly, trying to be amused*): Yes, I'm afraid I am. Fortunately, it's not serious.

DAVOS (*sceptical*): No? You don't tell me!

RALPH: The devil of it is that this is Saturday night. (*Embarked on a grievance*) I can't get in touch with the bank in London until Monday morning. This is the first time I've ever been in La Bandelette; they don't know me at the hotel; and my bill is due tomorrow. It'll be an unpleasant twenty-four hours until I can prove I've got plenty of money at home, but—

DAVOS (*bored*): You don't expect me to believe that, do you?

RALPH (*mildly*): I don't care what you believe, Mr. Davos. It happens to be true.

DAVOS: Look. Let's get down to business. How'd you like to make ten thousand francs?

RALPH: Doing what?

DAVOS: You said you were going back tomorrow. When and how?

RALPH: First plane tomorrow morning.

DAVOS: And how's your nerve?

RALPH: My *what?*

DAVOS: Your courage. Your intestinal fortitude. (*Sneering*) Ever test it?

RALPH (*hackles rising*): I don't know about my nerve, Mr. Davos. But you're putting a hell of a test on my patience.

DAVOS (*unruffled*): You needn't get on your high horse, old man. It doesn't impress me, and it won't help *you*. Do you want to earn ten thousand francs, or don't you? Yes or no?

RALPH (*snapping*): Yes, I do!

DAVOS: Right. (*Lowering his voice*) All I want you to do is take a certain object, put it in your suitcase, and carry it through the English customs for me. That's *all*.

RALPH: Oh? What am I to carry?

DAVOS: A bottle of—medicine. Yes, I said a bottle of medicine.

RALPH: What *is* this medicine?

DAVOS: It's not dope, if that's what you're thinking.

RALPH: But what *is* it?

DAVOS: I'm afraid that doesn't concern you. But *you're* not suspect; you could get this bottle past the customs authorities as easy as winking. What do you say?

RALPH: I don't like the sound of it, thanks.

DAVOS (*amused*): Afraid, eh?

RALPH: Now look here!

DAVOS: I know your sort, old man. I can read every thought in your head. You don't like me; you don't like my manners; you don't like anything. But this notecase! What *wouldn't* you give to have that! And wouldn't you like to take the job on, wouldn't you rather *like* to take it on just to wipe the sneer off my face?

RALPH: By the Lord, I believe I would!

DAVOS (*musingly*): Ten thousand francs. No fuss at the hotel. No scene. No embarrassment. A comfortable trip back on the day you'd arranged: all for a little harmless customsbilking! Think it over. (*He begins to whistle "Auprès de ma Blonde."*)

RALPH: Look here! (*Hesitates*) Where do I get this bottle of medicine?

DAVOS (*quickly*): Then you'll do it?

RALPH: Against my better judgement, yes.

DAVOS: Then listen to what you're to do. You'll leave here in about twenty minutes. . . .

RALPH: Alone?

DAVOS: Yes. We mustn't be seen together in public after this. You'll go to the address I give you; you'll get the medicine; and I'll tell you the rest later. (*Softly*) But don't try any funny business, old man.

RALPH: Meaning what?

DAVOS: There's a nice sharp knife—got that?—a nice sharp knife waiting for people who try funny business.

RALPH: I . . . What's the address?

DAVOS: Off the Avenue du Phare—that means Avenue of the Lighthouse—

RALPH: I have a working knowledge of French, thanks very much.

DAVOS: —there's a little cul-de-sac called the Square Rapp. Go to number four; it's a doctor's house: Dr. Lasalle. You can't miss it because there's always a light over the door.

RALPH: Is the doctor in on this?

DAVOS: That's none of your business either. Just ask for Mr. Davos's medicine. (*Chuckles*)

RALPH: Mr. Davos's medicine.

DAVOS: Which reminds me, old man, that we're neglecting our drinks. Good health!

RALPH (*mechanically*): Good health.

DAVOS: But remember—

RALPH (*sharply*): Remember what?

DAVOS: A nice sharp knife.

(*Music up.*)

NARRATOR: The Square Rapp, Avenue du Phare. (*Slight pause*) Lonely, now, as a deserted city. No noise here except the ceaseless pelting of the rain. A tiny square, half a dozen dingy, flat-roofed houses, shuttered and aloof. A white lamp above the door of number four, showing the brass nameplate of Dr. Edouard Lasalle. No other light except the beam of the great lighthouse that wheels overhead, turning the rain to silver. Silence to chill the nerves of a young man hesitating at the mouth of the square, ten minutes early for his meeting . . .

(*Sounds of rain.*)

RALPH (*muttering*): What's in the medicine bottle? What's *in* it? Why can't he carry it himself?

MARY (*calling*): Mr. Harvey!

RALPH (*unheeding*): It's not drugs, he says. But should be something like that, and if I get caught—

MARY: Mr. Harvey! Wait!

RALPH (*startled and nervous*): Who's there?

MARY (*fading on, rather breathless*): I tried to stop you before you left the casino, but I lost you in the crowd. Then I thought I saw you walking ahead of me, and—

RALPH: Aren't you—?

MARY: Yes, I'm Mary Stanhope. You're going to think I'm all kinds of a fool, following you like this. But—

RALPH: Look here, you're getting soaking wet. Come under the shelter of this shop door. Here!

MARY: You're pretty well drenched yourself.

RALPH (*struck by this*): Am I? Yes, I suppose I am.

MARY: I just wanted to tell you—don't do it!

RALPH: Don't do what?

MARY: Whatever it is you're up to! This man Davos is a criminal!

RALPH (*slight pause*): How do you know that?

MARY: The Prefect of the Police told me. He—oh! (*Gives a start*)

RALPH: Don't jump. It's only the lighthouse beam going round again.

MARY: I do jump. Every time. All white, with the rain against it . . .

RALPH: What's this about Ferdie Davos?

MARY: He's so clever, they've never been able to prove anything. But Monsieur Goron says they're certain Davos stole Lady Somebody's pearl necklace, worth thousands of pounds, from the Donjon Hotel. He can't get it out of the country, of course. . . .

RALPH: Did you say—pearl necklace?

MARY: Yes.

RALPH: But you couldn't hide a pearl necklace in a bottle of medicine.

MARY (*bewildered*): What's that?

RALPH: I mean, a custom's officer would only have to pick up the bottle, and shake it, and . . .

MARY: What on earth are you talking about?

RALPH: Listen, Mary. I've got the wind up. I'm scared green. Davos simply sat at the bar and looked at me. But his *eyes* when he started talking about a nice sharp knife . . .

MARY: Where's Davos now?

(*Off, faintly registering, we hear the whistling of "Auprès de ma Blonde."*)

RALPH: He's coming along the avenue now, towards this square!

MARY: Where's he going?

RALPH: You see that door across there? With the light over it and the doctor's name-plate on one side?

MARY: Well?

RALPH: He's . . . (*Breaking off*) Crouch back against the door here. Crouch back!

(*The whistling approaches, passes, and dies.*)

MARY (*whispering*): Did he see us?

RALPH (*whispering*): No, I'm pretty sure he didn't.

MARY: Where *is* he going?

RALPH: To the doctor's house there.

MARY: What are you going to *do*?

RALPH (*grimly*): I'm going to get you out of this mess, young lady, before it goes any further. I'm going to turn you round very firmly . . .

(*Off, a shriek of intense agony. Then a splash as of someone falling forward into very shallow water.*)

MARY (*crying out*): What was that? (*Pause. Then she starts to scream.*)

RALPH (*desperately*): Sh-h, for God's sake!

MARY (*panicky*): I'm all right. B-but—

RALPH (*dazed*): Do you see what I see?

MARY: Yes.

RALPH (*incredulously*): Davos lying flat on his face. His hands scratching at the pavement. *A knife in his back.*

MARY: What were you saying about sharp knives?

RALPH: But this isn't possible!

MARY: Why not?

RALPH: Because there's nobody near him. I took my eyes off him for only a fraction of a second, and—nobody came near him!

MARY: That's—true.

RALPH: Not a door opened. All these windows are shuttered. Nobody could have thrown the knife because we're standing in the mouth of the square. (*Breaking off*) Mary! Listen!

MARY: Yes?

RALPH: I'm going across to him. (*She starts to protest.*) When I get across there, you cut and run for it. Don't argue. Just do it. And—I'm grateful.

MARY: That doesn't matter! Only . . .

(*We hear his splashing footsteps.*)

RALPH: Davos . . . Davos! (*Footsteps stop.*) Davos, what happened? Here, let me raise you up. What's that notecase doing in your hand? Steady, old man! Don't jerk! I'm a friend. Give me the notecase. I . . .

(*A noise from* DAVOS, *something between a cry and a moan. Then a splash as though the body has fallen back inert.*)

RALPH: *Davos!*

GORON (*shouting, off*): *Qui va là? Qu'est-ce se passe?*

RALPH (*jumping*): Who spoke then?

GORON (*suavely grim*): *I* spoke, young man. Don't move, please! I can see you under the light.

RALPH: Who are you?

GORON: I happen, young man, to be the Prefect of Police.

RALPH: Prefect of . . . This man Davos! He's been stabbed in the back!

GORON: Yes, so I observe.

RALPH: I think he's—well, I think he's dead.

GORON: That also is evident.

RALPH: By the way. This notecase I have here. It's—it's his.

GORON (*drily*): Indeed. And full of money, eh?

RALPH: Yes.

GORON: He offered it to you, I suppose?

RALPH: No! Of course not! He . . . (*Suddenly realizing*) Wait a minute! (*Slight pause*) You don't think *I* killed him? (*Music up.*)

NARRATOR: The consulting room of Dr. Lasalle at three o'clock in the morning. A consulting room—with its glass-fronted cabinets, its operating-table—now turned into a temporary police headquarters. Behind the desk, sitting in the doctor's chair,

M. Jean Goron with an *agent de police* on either side . . .

GORON: For the last time, young man, *will* you tell me the truth?

RALPH: For the last time, sir, I *have* told you the truth!

MARY: It's true, Monsieur Goron! Every word of it!

GORON (*politely*): Will you forgive me, Miss Stanhope, if I refuse to believe one syllable you utter about this young man?

MARY: But I saw it! I was there!

GORON: Pardon me, mademoiselle. You followed him, as I followed you. You were not there when he—

RALPH: I tell you, I didn't kill him!

GORON: Will you explain, please, how this notecase got into your hand if you didn't steal it?

RALPH: He had it in his own hand. I took it from him when I tried to lift him up.

GORON: *Davos* took it out of his own pocket, then? Why?

RALPH: I don't know.

GORON: Consider your own statement. You saw Davos. Yes! You saw him in good light. Yes! Yet you say nobody attacked him?

RALPH: I do.

GORON: Now look at the weapon. Sergeant Mercier!

(MERCIER *is an agent de police.*)

MERCIER: *Oui, monsieur?*

GORON: The knife, if you please.

MERCIER: *Bien, monsieur.*

GORON: Don't be afraid, mademoiselle. All the blood has been cleaned off. Do you know, young man, what this is?

RALPH: It looks like a carving knife.

GORON: A dinner carving knife. Yes. Polished metal handle, very heavy blade. This knife is—what you call—awkward.

MARY: Can't you put it *away?*

GORON: It could not have been thrown. You yourself admit it was *not* thrown, since you stood at the entrance of the square.

RALPH: That's absolutely true.

GORON: You say this knife was not used as a dagger in the hand of an assassin?

RALPH: Yes, I do.

GORON: But at the same time it was not thrown?

RALPH: Right.

GORON (*powerfully restrained*): It follows, then, that I seek an invisible murderer?

(*Door rapidly opens and closes.* DR. LASALLE, *who has a deep hollow voice, as though speaking with his chin drawn in, approaches.*)

LASALLE (*drawn up*): Monsieur le Prefet. Pour la dernière fois, et pour protéger mon reputation professionel—

GORON: Please. Please. For the sake of my . . . (*bitterly*) . . . friends here, you will speak English.

LASALLE: I am Dr. Lasalle.

GORON (*wearily*): Yes, dear doctor. I know that.

LASALLE: And I come to ask why my house is invaded.

GORON: Because this young man tells us—a clear lie—that he came here to get a bottle of medicine for Davos.

LASALLE (*taken aback*): But—this is not a lie!

GORON: *Not a lie?*

LASALLE: No. Here is the medicine. I have it here now.

GORON: Give it to me, please. Give it to me!

LASALLE: As you wish, monsieur. I know nothing of this Davos, except that he consulted me for—

GORON: "One tablespoonful every three hours." I uncork it—so. I taste it—so. I pour it out on the floor. . . . (*Splashing*) This *is* cough medicine and nothing else!

LASALLE: But of course it is! Why do you pour it on the floor?

GORON (*formally*): Messieurs et mesdames. I go mad. (*Bursting out*) Slowly I go mad!

MARY: Please, Monsieur Goron. In another minute you'll be foaming at the mouth!

GORON (*controlling himself*): We have here three objects which make no sense. One sharp knife. One notecase, the property of the late Davos. One bottle of medicine. You cannot tell me he offered ten thousand francs to have a bottle of cough medicine carried through the English customs.

RALPH: Excuse me, sir; will you let *me* talk? Will you let the person who's being questioned get a word in edgeways?

GORON: Well?

RALPH: Don't blow up, sir. But . . . that isn't Ferdie Davos's notecase.

GORON (*sharply*): *What's that?*

RALPH: I was sitting with him at the bar. He kept waving a notecase at me, and saying didn't I wish it was mine. But I'll swear his case was a lighter colour than that.

MERCIER (*gruffly*): *Monsieur le Prefet.*

GORON: Yes, Sergeant Mercier?

MERCIER: This at least is true. When we have searched the dead man's body, we find another of these cases. Yes.

GORON (*groping*): Two notecases. A knife with a polished metal handle and a heavy blade. Now if this medicine had been pills, not cough medicine . . . (*Bursting out*) Oh, beautiful deviltry!

MARY: What *is* it? Have you got an idea?

GORON: Yes, mademoiselle. Distinctly I have an idea.

MARY: Well?

GORON: I begin to see how Dr. Lasalle committed this murder. (*Knife-chord.*)

LASALLE (*bursting out*): *Qu'est-ce qu'il dit? Qu'est-ce qu'il dit?*

GORON: Suppose you want to smuggle a stolen necklace out of the country. You can't hide it in liquid medicine, no. *But*—

RALPH: But what?

GORON: You can take the necklace to pieces. You can cover each bead with a sugar coating like a medical pill. You can pour them into a bottle. You can write a neat label and have your dupe carry them without suspicion. That—believe me!—was the original bottle. And, when Dr. Lasalle kills his partner Davos, he gives us this false bottle to throw us off the track.

LASALLE: All this is lies! I kill nobody! I can prove it!

RALPH: Sir, he's right.

GORON: You think so?

MARY: He never went near that man.

GORON: He didn't have to.

RALPH: I swear the door of this house never opened! Neither did a window!

GORON: It didn't have to open.

RALPH (*pleading*): Listen, sir! There are only four directions from which the murderer could have got at him. North, south, east, and west. Four faces like the points of a compass. Which direction was it?

GORON: None of them.

RALPH (*wildly*): Are you crazy, or am I?

GORON: Attend now and I tell you. You yourself arrived here early. Yes?

RALPH: Yes. Ten minutes early. But—

GORON: Davos has meant to be here before you. But his partner, the good doctor, has other plans for him. With Davos dead, you would walk into the trap and get the blame. Just before Davos is to arrive, Dr. Lasalle goes softly up to the roof of this house: a flat roof. In one hand he has the knife, in the other a well-filled notecase. He drops the notecase to the pavement below, under a light. Davos comes along, and . . . *well?* What would *you* do if you saw a case full of money lying at your feet?

RALPH: I'd—I'd bend over and pick it up.

MARY: You mean—?

GORON: Exactly. You would bend over so that your back was parallel with the ground. Dr. Lasalle has only to drop the knife—stretch out his hand and drop it. You took your eyes off Davos for a second. But you wouldn't have seen this even if you had been looking at him. Because a wall of rain, turned to silver by the beam of the lighthouse, hid the fall of a blade with a bright metal handle, and . . .

RALPH: *He's going for the knives in that cabinet. Grab him!*
   (*A cry, scufflings, the crash of glass, and a thud.*)

MERCIER (*gruffly*): Sois sage, docteur! Sois sage!
   (*Music up.*)

October 19, 1944.

"Just how far does any man trust his wife?" asked the American narrator in introducing this play; "or his fiancée either for that matter?" The question is so compelling that Carr built several works around it. Two versions of this script survive: the British "Vampire Tower" and the American "Will You Walk into My Parlor?" The plot development is the same, but the names of the characters differ and most of the speeches are rewritten. Carr's 1944 novel *Till Death Do Us Part* also uses some of the same ideas. Carr never posed the question more effectively than in "Vampire Tower," with its contrast between the hearty normality of an English fête and the tale of a tortured soul.

Vampire Tower

THE CHARACTERS:

Sir Harvey Drake	Of Layton Hall
Alan Drake	His nephew
Barbara Morell	Alan's fiancée
Dr. George Grimaud	Authority on murder
Major Selden	Chief Constable

Setting: Kent, 1930s.

NARRATOR: The vampire, according to legend, is a monster who feeds on the blood of the living. But there are many kinds of vampire, aren't there? I remember one such case not many years ago which has kept me chuckling ever since. Come now, on a drowsy summer afternoon before the war, to a charity bazaar in the grounds of a country house in Kent. Layton Hall is the home of Sir Harvey Drake, always ready in the cause of charity. There's the dark red brick of the hall, rising above the oak trees. There are the stalls and tents of the bazaar—almost deserted now, as the sky darkens with summer storm and a rising wind begins to flap and thrum among the belling tents. . . . (*Thunder*) There's the fortune-teller's tent, gaudy in purple and gold. There's the miniature shooting gallery, presided over by Sir Harvey Drake himself. And, as the sky darkens still more, you can see only two persons crossing that lawn. One is a young man, Sir Harvey's nephew. The other . . .

(*Thunder.*)

BARBARA: Alan, it's going to pour with rain in a minute. Hadn't we better run for the house?

ALAN: Not just yet, Barbara. (*Mock serious*) And it strikes me, my dear, you've been carrying discourtesy too far.

BARBARA (*surprised*): Discourtesy? I have?

ALAN: You've been engaged to me for a matter of six days, six hours, and umpty-umph minutes. My uncle approves, with loud cheers—

BARBARA (*quickly*): Does he, Alan? Does he really?

ALAN: —and yet you've never been near him to ask for his blessing. I call that discourtesy.

BARBARA (*very seriously*): It wasn't because I didn't want to see him. Don't you *know* that?

ALAN (*surprised*): Easy, Barbara. I was only joking.

BARBARA: It's just—happened like that. There hasn't been any opportunity.

ALAN: There's an opportunity now. He won't leave that shooting range until the storm breaks. And, as an added inducement, look over there beyond it.

BARBARA: At what?

ALAN: At the purple and gold tent with the light inside it. That's the fortune-teller's. Didn't you say you wanted to get your fortune told?

BARBARA (*wryly amused*): Yes, I'm afraid I do.

ALAN: *Afraid* you do?

BARBARA: I know it's all rubbish, but I can't resist getting my fortune told over and over again. Alan, who *is* the fortune-teller?

ALAN: There's his sign on the tent. "The Great Omar. Palmist and Crystal Gazer. Sees all, knows all."

BARBARA: I mean, who is he in real life? It can't be anybody from the village, or we'd all know it was a fake.

ALAN: Why not ask my uncle? He's signalling to us now, and . . .

(SIR HARVEY DRAKE *is elderly, with an amiable and hearty voice.*)

DRAKE: Hallo, there! You two! Come here!

BARBARA (*suddenly*): Please, Alan! We don't . . . we don't *have* to go there, do we?

ALAN: Go where?

BARBARA: To that shooting-range. I *hate* guns!

ALAN (*puzzled*): But we can't insult the old boy, my dear. What's wrong? You've met him often enough before. (*Calling*) Coming, sir!

BARBARA: I'm sorry. Only—I suppose they're saying all sorts of things about me in the village.

ALAN: About you? What should they be saying?

BARBARA (*with intensity*): Listen, Alan. You *know* I love you?

ALAN (*seriously*): I hope so, my dear. I rather think you'd have my death on your conscience if you didn't.

DRAKE: Now then, you two!

ALAN: All right, Uncle Harvey.

DRAKE: Come up to the counter here—how do I look as a showman?—and no more nonsense about it. I just want to tell this nephew of mine, Barbara, what a lucky fellow he is.

BARBARA: Thank you, Sir Harvey. We . . .

DRAKE (*expansively*): And you, young woman! Give me your hand.

BARBARA (*catching his tone*): Then you approve of me, Sir Harvey?

DRAKE: I'm not altogether sure I do approve.

BARBARA: Oh? Any reason?

DRAKE: You come here only six months ago. You turn the head of every male in the district. You deprive Alan of what little sanity he's got left . . .

ALAN: I cheerfully admit it.

DRAKE: . . . and make all the fond mothers foam at the mouth. Damme, my girl, how do you do it? Are you a demon in disguise, or what?

(*Thunder. The rushing of wind, with flapping canvas, begins faintly and grows louder.*)

BARBARA: I'm awfully grateful, Sir Harvey. But it *is* going to storm in a minute, and we hoped to see the fortune-teller before we left. If you wouldn't mind letting go my hand . . . ?

DRAKE (*mock serious*): No, you don't, my girl. Not a bit of it!

BARBARA: You won't let me go?

DRAKE (*jocosely*): Not until you've patronized *this* charity. As a preparation to polishing off your husband after marriage, why not try a few rounds with a rifle?

BARBARA: No! Please!

DRAKE (*unheeding*): Now here's a neat little model. Winchester 61. Twenty-two calibre hammerless. Try it.

BARBARA: I can't do it, Sir Harvey. I know it sounds stupid and silly to say that. But it's not the rifle, really. It's . . . it's anything having to do with—death.

ALAN: With death?

BARBARA: I mean, anything that suggests death. Ever since I was a child, I've never even been able to look at a dead person in a coffin. It frightens me.

ALAN: But nobody's going to die. Just blaze away and see if you can hit the target.

BARBARA: All right. If you insist. But . . .

ALAN: Your left hand out here, like this . . . head down. Left eye along the sights, and . . .

DRAKE: *Look out!*

(*Rifle shot, and sharp pop of exploding glass.*)

ALAN (*indulgently*): No, Barbara. You've hit the electric light in the roof. You're not supposed to aim at that.

DRAKE: Look here, my lad. Speaking of sudden death . . .

ALAN: Easy, sir! Easy, now!

DRAKE: If that's her style of target shooting, damme if I don't crawl out from under this counter and stand behind her. Make way!

BARBARA (*desperately*): Here's the rifle, Alan. I'm sorry but I can't go on with this.

ALAN (*worried*): I'm the one to be sorry. If I'd known it was going to upset you like this . . .

BARBARA: That's all right. It doesn't matter.

DRAKE (*soothingly*): You run along and see the fortune-teller, my dear. He'll only admit one at a time.

ALAN: Yes. Go ahead. I'll wait for you. (*Slight pause while wind rises*) She keeps getting these nervous fits, and I don't like it. What's more, I hope the fortune-telling doesn't take long.

DRAKE: Why so?

ALAN: The sky's getting as black as pitch, and this wind is going to blow all your tents into the next county.

DRAKE (*comfortably*): The tents are pretty securely pegged, my lad. I think we can risk it.

ALAN: It's so dark that . . . look there!

DRAKE: Where?

ALAN: At the fortune-teller's tent. He's got a light inside, and you can see his shadow against the tent. There's Barbara going in . . . she's sitting down across the table from him. . . .

DRAKE (*confidentially, amused*): By the way, do you happen to know who the fortune-teller is?

ALAN: No. I was going to ask you.

DRAKE (*chuckles*): I'll tell you a little secret. He's probably the greatest living authority on murder.

ALAN: On *what?*

DRAKE: On murder. Ever hear of Dr. George Grimaud, the Home Office Pathologist?

ALAN: You don't mean—?

DRAKE (*pleased*): He's the chap who appears for the prosecution at murder trials, with the corpse's insides in a glass jar, and tells you the cause of death.

ALAN: But what the devil's he doing *here?*

DRAKE: He came down to see John Selden—you know; the Chief Constable—and I asked him to be our fortune-teller. He's one of those glittering-eye blokes. And in a turban, with brown paint on his face. . . .

ALAN (*sharply*): Wait a minute!

DRAKE: Is anything wrong?

ALAN: What's he saying to Barbara? Look at the shadows! (*A heavier gust of wind and flapping canvas.*)

DRAKE: Confound this wind! There goes my hat!

ALAN (*intent*): It's like watching a shadow-play against a screen. Barbara's jumped up and backed away from him. He's pointing a finger at her. She seems to be running out of the tent! Running as though . . . Barbara! Barbara! (*Sharp, brief musical bridge*) Barbara, what is it? What's wrong?

BARBARA (*with an effort*): I don't understand, Alan. There's nothing wrong.

ALAN: What was he saying to you?

BARBARA: Nothing at all! I mean, only the usual nonsense about a happy life and a little illness; but nothing serious.

ALAN: Then why were you so frightened?

BARBARA: Was I frightened? I don't think so.

ALAN: I'm sorry, my dear, but I saw your shadow on the wall of that tent. (*Grimly*) Here; you'd better hold this rifle. I think I'll go in and have *my* fortune told.

BARBARA (*crying out*): Alan, you mustn't!

ALAN: Why not?

BARBARA: I—I felt a drop of rain on my head. Hadn't we better get to the house?

ALAN: You go on up to the house. I want to see this very curious fortune-teller.

BARBARA: Alan! Please!

(*Heavy rain blots out the noise of the wind for a second or two before* ALAN *speaks again.*)

ALAN: I say! Fortune-teller! May I come in?

(DR. GRIMAUD *has a heavy middle-aged voice which intones his words in a deliberately mysterious and guttural way.*)

GRIMAUD: You may. Please to enter.

ALAN: Thank you.

GRIMAUD: Sit down in the chair opposite me. First tell me the date of your birth. Then look at the crystal on the table in front of you.

ALAN: Excuse me, Dr. Grimaud; do you mind if we drop the mumbo-jumbo?

GRIMAUD (*relaxing, in ordinary English*): As a matter of fact, young man, I'd prefer to. It's been something of a strain, talking like Hamlet's father's ghost.

ALAN (*grimly*): I imagine it has.

GRIMAUD: I must get up and stretch my legs. (*Deep breath; then harshly*) And, to tell you the truth, I've had—a bit of a shock.

ALAN: *You've* had a shock? What about Miss Morell?

GRIMAUD: Miss *who?*

ALAN: Miss Barbara Morell. The girl who was just in here. My fiancée.

GRIMAUD (*sharply*): Did you say . . . fiancée?

ALAN: Yes, of course. Why not?

GRIMAUD (*restraining himself*): Tell me, Mr. . . . ?

ALAN: My name is Drake, Alan Drake.

GRIMAUD: Tell me, Mr. Drake. Has Miss—Miss Morell lived here in the village for very long?

ALAN: No. Only about six months. Why?

GRIMAUD: And how long have you been engaged to her? (*Sharply*) Believe me, I have a reason for asking that. How long have you been engaged?

ALAN: It'll be a week tomorrow.

GRIMAUD: A week tomorrow! Has she by any chance invited you to dinner at her house tomorrow night?

ALAN: I . . .

GRIMAUD (*fiercely*): Has she?

ALAN: Yes. As a matter of fact, she has. But . . .

GRIMAUD (*suavely*): A cynic like myself, Mr. Drake, should enjoy this position. He should relish human folly as I relish it by playing fortune-teller. But I'm afraid actually I don't enjoy it at all. (*Grimly*) Do you know who this young lady, this "Barbara Morell," really is? Of course you don't. *She is* . . .

(*Rifle shot. Grimaud cries out.*)

ALAN: Dr. Grimaud! (*Slight pause*) *Dr. Grimaud!*

(*Crash of falling table; thud of body.*)

BARBARA (*calling*): Sir Harvey, I couldn't help it! But Alan shouldn't have given me this rifle to hold. All I did was touch the trigger by accident. (*Innocently*) I—I do hope I haven't hit anything.

(*Music up.*)

NARRATOR: An unfortunate accident, as everyone agreed. The bullet hole in the tent wall; the fallen body and the fallen crystal. It was late that evening, at the Feathers Inn outside the village, that a white-faced young man slipped through the side door of the inn, and up the staircase, and along the passage outside the bedrooms, and knocked at a certain door.

(*Knocking.*)

GRIMAUD (*muffled*): Yes? Come in.

ALAN (*amazed*): Good God, Dr. Grimaud! I thought—

GRIMAUD: Come in here and close the door! Quickly!

ALAN: But—you're sitting up in bed.

GRIMAUD: And taking nourishment, thanks.

ALAN: I nearly jumped out of my skin when I heard your voice. They said . . .

GRIMAUD: They said I was unconscious and not expected to live. Yes. That was what I told them to say.

ALAN: How seriously *are* you hurt?

GRIMAUD: A flesh wound under the left shoulder-blade. Devilish painful; nothing more.

ALAN: Look here, Dr. Grimaud. Poor Barbara is nearly frantic. She thinks she killed you. Let me ring her up and . . .

GRIMAUD (*sharply*): Stay away from that telephone!

ALAN: But why?

GRIMAUD: I want you to sit down very quietly, while the curtains are drawn and nobody can hear us. I want to ask you what you know about "Miss Barbara Morell."

ALAN (*bracing himself*): Listen, Dr. Grimaud. If you're trying to tell me Barbara is . . . well! a criminal of some kind . . .

GRIMAUD: Go on.

ALAN: It's fantastic! You've only got to look at her. She's got plenty of money, a collection of jewelry worth thousands . . .

GRIMAUD: Yes. Hasn't she?

ALAN: Then what are you getting at?

GRIMAUD: To the psychologist, young man, this lady presents an interesting problem. She looks, as you say, like something out of a stained-glass window. Her kindliness is perfectly genuine. Her innocence is perfectly genuine. The only trouble is . . .

ALAN: Well?

GRIMAUD: She's a poisoner.

(*Knife-chord.*)

ALAN (*loudly*): Are you out of your mind?

GRIMAUD (*quietly*): You know I'm not.

ALAN: You said—?

GRIMAUD: A murderess, young man. Her favorite weapon is antimony, or tartar emetic. Rather slow and horribly painful, but that's what the poisoner likes.

ALAN (*wildly*): I don't believe it!

GRIMAUD: My dear sir, don't take *my* word. I've got in touch with Major Selden, the Chief Constable. There'll be a man down from London tomorrow with photographs and fingerprints.

ALAN: You don't mean—she's been on trial?

GRIMAUD: Yes. Once. On other occasions when friends of hers died . . .

ALAN: Other occasions?

GRIMAUD: Four or five, I believe. Would you care to hear about the trial?

ALAN: No! Yes! I . . .

GRIMAUD: She was then using the name of "Jane Jordan." Ever hear of it?

ALAN: Yes, I do seem to remember . . .

GRIMAUD: She came to live in a village very much like this one. She became engaged to a young man very much like you. Exactly a week after the engagement, she invited him to dine at her house. He came home from that dinner and died of antimony poisoning.

ALAN: And what was the jury's verdict?

GRIMAUD: They acquitted her.

ALAN: But if she wasn't guilty . . .

GRIMAUD: My dear sir! They acquitted her because we couldn't show *how* the poison was administered.

ALAN (*hesitating*): Meaning . . . what?

GRIMAUD: Miss Jane Jordan, or Barbara Morell, employed a staff of three servants.

ALAN: She still does.

GRIMAUD: Those servants prepared every bit of food or drink that was taken at dinner. There was always someone in the room while they were eating. The defence proved it was absolutely impossible for her to have given him poison.

ALAN: Then what more do you want?

GRIMAUD: The man died. Four others had already died in the same way.

ALAN: Then how did she do it?

GRIMAUD (*flatly*): I don't know.

ALAN (*desperately*): But listen, Dr. Grimaud! The *motive* for all this . . . ?

GRIMAUD (*quietly*): Will you get it out of your head, young man, that the motive for murder is always money, or revenge, or a love affair? The poisoner belongs to a race apart. She can't help herself.

ALAN (*bewildered*): Can't help herself?

GRIMAUD: Here's a human soul . . . say "mind" if you like the word better . . . locked up in its own tower. Secret and apart and impenetrable. Existing only to gloat when it draws the life from fellow creatures. It's a modern version, the true version, of the old vampire legend. And when it takes to poisoning by antimony . . .

ALAN: Answer me one question. Was any poison ever traced to— to Barbara?

GRIMAUD: No. It's true she always had an elaborate wall safe in her bedroom.

ALAN: There's a wall safe in the house she's got now. The combination opens to the letters of her own surname.

GRIMAUD (*sharply*): Did you ever see inside that safe?

ALAN: Once or twice. But how in blazes should I recognize antimony if I saw it?

GRIMAUD: Antimony is a colourless and tasteless liquid. (*Quickly*) Are you *sure* you never . . . ?

ALAN (*bursting out*): I tell you, the whole thing's fantastic! I'm
     going to ring up Barbara and ask her point-blank . . .

GRIMAUD: There's the telephone. I can't stop you. But I'd rather
     hoped you'd help me with a little experiment.

ALAN: What experiment?

GRIMAUD: You're to be this lady's next victim. Hadn't you
     guessed?

ALAN: I . . .

GRIMAUD: Come now, young man. Don't say you hadn't thought
     of it.

ALAN (*badgered*): Not until now, but . . .

GRIMAUD: But you still doubt the evidence?

ALAN: I'm afraid I do.

GRIMAUD (*politely*): Then of course you wouldn't mind acting as
     stalking horse.

ALAN: How do you mean?

GRIMAUD: The lady thinks I'm unconscious and dying. If I could
     be hidden somewhere in that house, and watch her in action
     when she tries to poison you tomorrow night . . . (*Tele-
     phone rings sharply.*) Don't jump, Mr. Drake! It's only the
     telephone.

ALAN: Look here, Dr. Grimaud; I'm not going through with this.
     Suppose it's somebody who looks like Barbara? Suppose
     there's been a mistake?

GRIMAUD: Would you mind answering the phone. I'm supposed
     to be dying.
         (*Phone picked up.*)

ALAN (*confusedly*): Hello? Who's speaking, please?

BARBARA (*on filter, startled*): Alan? Is that you?

ALAN: *Barbara!*

GRIMAUD (*fiercely muttering*): Put your hand over the mouth-
     piece of the phone!

ALAN (*muttering*): Well?

GRIMAUD: The game's in your hands now. You can give the
     whole show away—or you can help trap a murderess.

ALAN (*desperately*): Suppose there *has* been a mistake?

GRIMAUD: Suppose there hasn't?

ALAN: I tell you, I'm going to marry her!

GRIMAUD: Even if she *is* a poisoner?

BARBARA: What on earth are you mumbling about? I can't hear
     you.

ALAN: It's nothing, Barbara. There's—there's something wrong
with the phone.

BARBARA: Alan, listen. I've been talking to Sir Harvey and the
Chief Constable. They say I'll not really get into trouble
over . . . you know . . . what happened with the rifle; because, of course, anybody could see it was an accident.

ALAN: Of course.

BARBARA: But they've been telling me this fortune-teller was really Dr. George Grimaud, the Home Office Pathologist. Did
you know that?

ALAN: Yes, Barbara. I know it.

BARBARA: I *thought* I'd seen him somewhere before. It was . . .
it was at the trial, I expect.

ALAN (*hoarsely*): What trial?

BARBARA: Just a trial where they couldn't prove anything. Hasn't
anybody . . . mentioned it to you?

GRIMAUD (*grimly*): Well, Mr. Drake?

ALAN: *What* trial, Barbara?

BARBARA: It doesn't matter, dear. I'll explain tomorrow night.
What I really rang up about . . . how *is* Dr. Grimaud? He's
getting better, isn't he? He's not really going to die?

GRIMAUD: Make your choice, Mr. Drake.

ALAN: He's . . . he's . . . I mean—

BARBARA: Speak up, Alan. I can't hear you.

GRIMAUD: If I have a chance to watch her, I may be able to see
how she administers poison under the eyes of witnesses. If
not, you can die in convulsions and still think she looks like
a saint. As a student of murder I'm very, very interested;
and by all that's holy, the whole thing depends on you.
What do you say?

ALAN: Barbara.

BARBARA: Yes, Alan?

ALAN: I'm afraid Grimaud's still unconscious. But—I shall be
there for dinner tomorrow night.

BARBARA (*slight pause*): All my love, Alan!

ALAN (*swallowing*): All mine, Barbara. Good night.
(*Music up.*)

NARRATOR: You will find in the records that the home of Miss
Barbara Morell was a very modern house, staffed with three
servants. On a fine summer evening . . . a time for open
windows, and iced drinks, and light meals that are not too

difficult to eat . . . Barbara Morell and Alan Drake sat before dinner in a long, dusky drawing-room with French windows giving on a flagged terrace. And as twilight deepened on that drowsy evening . . .

(*Faint, distant church bell.*)

BARBARA (*quietly*): Alan.

ALAN (*on edge*): Yes, my dear?

BARBARA: What's wrong with you tonight?

ALAN: There's nothing wrong with me, Barbara.

BARBARA: You can't sit still. You keep looking round the room, and out of the windows, and up at the ceiling, as though . . .

ALAN: As though—what?

BARBARA: A moment ago, you know, I could have sworn I heard somebody moving about in the front bedroom upstairs.

ALAN (*quickly*): That's impossible! I mean, there's nobody here except ourselves and the servants. Maybe one of the servants?

BARBARA: No. They're downstairs.

ALAN: Anyway, does it matter?

BARBARA: No, I suppose not. Don't you like your gin and ginger ale?

ALAN: Very much, thanks.

BARBARA: But you're not drinking it.

(*Slight pause. Deep breath from* ALAN.)

ALAN (*defiantly*): There! Down the hatch at one go! How's that?

BARBARA: Would you care for another?

ALAN: No, thanks. One will be enough.

BARBARA: I'm sure it will.

ALAN (*jumping*): What do you mean by that?

BARBARA (*earnestly*): Only that you're not yourself tonight, Alan. You haven't been yourself all evening.

ALAN: It strikes me you're a bit on edge too.

BARBARA: Yes, I suppose I am. And yet I was thinking how quiet it is tonight. Quiet and peaceful and remote from the world. With the twilight coming down and the trees turning to shadows. As though we might go to sleep now and never wake up again.

ALAN: A person who did that might as well be dead.

BARBARA: Yes, that's what I mean. There have been times in the past week when I wished *I* were dead.

ALAN: Why?

BARBARA: Because I've got a confession to make to you. Did you ever hear of a woman named Jane Jordan?

ALAN (*suddenly*): Barbara, wait!

BARBARA: Wait for what?

ALAN: I thought I could go through with this, but I can't. (*Fiercely*) If you've got anything to tell me, I don't want to hear it! Do you understand? I don't want to hear it!

BARBARA: But you've *got* to hear it, my darling. *Did* you ever hear of Jane Jordan?

ALAN: Yes. But don't say any more! There's a—

BARBARA: She was accused of poisoning a young man who was in love with her. It took seven hours for him to die, and they had to give him opiates because he was screaming so much. But that was the odd thing.

ALAN: What was?

BARBARA: The victim himself said she couldn't have given him any poison. And the defence proved that she didn't prepare or touch or even go near any of the things he ate or drank.

ALAN: And was that true?

BARBARA: Perfectly true.

ALAN: Then she didn't kill him?

BARBARA: Oh, yes, she did.

ALAN: Barbara, let's turn on the lights. It's getting so dark I can't see you.

BARBARA: No, dear. We won't turn on the lights. Not just yet.

ALAN: Why not?

BARBARA: Because I don't *want* you to see me. I'm bad stock. And the morbid idea that's been occurring to me . . . (*starts to laugh*) . . . is that I could kill *you* just as she killed *her* victim. (*Seriously*) I could, you know. Quite easily.

ALAN: I don't think you could, unless you happen to be a magician.

BARBARA: You say that because you don't know the secret, Alan. You might be dying at this very minute.

ALAN: Dying . . . how?

BARBARA: The police forgot that Jane Jordan's house was a modern house. Like this one.

ALAN: A modern house? What's that got to do with it?

BARBARA: They forgot the electric refrigerator. And the ice

cubes. (*Crash of breaking glass*) Don't drop your glass, Alan!

ALAN (*fiercely*): Get on with it! What did Jane Jordan do?

BARBARA: You can buy a poison called antimony as a colourless liquid. Pour it into a drawer of ice cubes and let the water freeze. Offer your victim gin and ginger ale, which needs ice on a hot day. Somebody else prepared the drink in the kitchen, so they all swear you never came near it and couldn't have poisoned it. Isn't it *terribly* easy?

(*Three blasts of a police whistle.*)

VOICE (*calling*): All right, boys! Cover the house. There'll be no getting away *this* time!

BARBARA (*terrified*): *What was that?*

ALAN: It sounded like Major Selden. The Chief Constable.

BARBARA: It *is* Major Selden. He's outside the French window now. He . . .

(SELDEN, *in his early forties, has a brisk, military, no-nonsense voice.*)

SELDEN (*grimly*): As a matter of fact, Miss Morell, he's in the room. I'm sorry to intrude like this; I'm sorry to break up a pleasant little evening; but I've got an arrest to make.

BARBARA (*crying out*): Alan!

ALAN: You'll never make that arrest, Major Selden.

SELDEN (*pulled up*): I won't make the arrest? And why the devil not?

ALAN: Because I refuse to testify. I don't care *what* she's done! I'll swear I drank the damn stuff voluntarily!

SELDEN (*with restraint*): Would you mind telling me, Mr. Drake, just what in blazes you're talking about?

BARBARA: Wait a minute! I think *I* know. Alan, listen to me! It's my own fault. I let my nerves run away with me. But when I mentioned Jane Jordan . . .

ALAN: Well?

BARBARA: You didn't think I was talking about myself, did you? I was talking about heredity.

ALAN: Heredity?

BARBARA: When a thing like that is in your own family . . . is in your own flesh and blood . . . don't you see how it can make you morbid and nearly drive you mad? Don't you understand why I had to tell you, and get it off my conscience at last?

ALAN: Look here, Barbara; what *are* you trying to tell me?

BARBARA: Jane Jordan was my elder sister. She died in Canada two years ago.

ALAN: Will somebody wake me up out of this nightmare? Major Selden here says he came to make an arrest.

SELDEN: That's right. And the man I'm after, of course, is the imposter who calls himself Dr. George Grimaud.

(*Knife-chord.*)

BARBARA (*blankly*): Who *calls* himself Dr. Grimaud?

SELDEN: He's a slippery customer, but we've nailed him this time. Where is he now?

ALAN: As a matter of fact, he's upstairs in the front room.

SELDEN: In the same room with a safe full of valuable jewellery? He hasn't by any chance got the combination of that safe?

ALAN: My God! He has. I gave it to him.

BARBARA: But what's he doing here? Who *is* he?

SELDEN (*as though quoting*): "Samuel Drexel, alias Samuel Marsden, alias Soapy Sam." He's the cleverest jewel-thief out of jail. His speciality is learning everything about the people in a community, and then telling artistic lies . . .

ALAN (*thoughtfully*): Artistic lies.

SELDEN: . . . so that he worms into your confidence and gets into a position to lift the best jewellery without even having to open a window. He even had the nerve to play "Dr. Grimaud" in front of the police, and he might have got away with it if it hadn't been for that rifle accident. We phoned London to explain, and found that the real Dr. Grimaud never left town. (*Suddenly realizing*) By the way, Miss Morell, Mr. Drake. What sort of ghost story has he been telling *you?*

(*Music up.*)

May 11, 1944.

When John Dickson Carr chose a story by another author to adapt for the radio, he usually revised the original so much that it became his own work. For example, Carr rewrote Edgar Allan Poe's "The Tell-Tale Heart" to add a rational explanation for the heartbeats, and stories by G. K. Chesterton, Arthur Conan Doyle, Robert Louis Stevenson, Ambrose Bierce, and Melville Davisson Post also appeared with Carr's stamp. For this book, we have chosen "The Devil's Manuscript," based (with many changes) on Bierce's "The Suitable Surroundings."

In Carr's work anything can be deadly . . . even a manuscript.

The Devil's Manuscript

THE CHARACTERS:

Dr. Daniel Shaw	Who tells the story
Roy Saunders	Who visits the Brede House
Jenny Ames	Who accompanies him
Willard Marsh	A solicitor
James Colston	Who writes ghost stories

Setting: Weyford, an English seaside town, 1934.

NARRATOR: Tonight's story belongs to Dr. Daniel Shaw, with his big head and his cropped beard, spending the twilight of his years at the seaside town of Weyford. And, as we peer with him at a certain evil document, we trust we shall keep our promise to bring you . . . (*Knife-chord*) *An Appointment with Fear!*

(DR. DANIEL SHAW *has a slow, heavy, kindly voice; his age is about sixty; he is perturbed, toiling as though to make difficult things clear.*)

SHAW: How did it happen, you ask? Can a manuscript, a mere story, strike the life out of a man's body? (*Slight pause*) This is not the record of a haunted house. I wish it were! But I ask you to think of the Brede House, hidden away in deep country lanes some miles from Weyford. Not a very pretentious place, not even very old. A square Victorian house of grey stone, with long sash-windows reaching to the ground; long deserted, long fallen to ruin. A rotted skull of a house: its shutters fallen, its windows defaced, its vast grounds overgrown. That's how it looked ten years ago, when it happened. The first part of the story belongs to a pair of innocents—Roy Saunders, aged twenty; and Jenny Ames, aged eighteen—driving home from a dance that summer night. He in the glory of a new dinner jacket, she in a sophisticated gown borrowed from her elder sister. Driving home in father's car; driving home to Weyford through the country lanes at that drugged hour of the night when the headlamps shine drowsily on a white road . . .

(*A motorcar engine begins to cough and miss.*)

JENNY: Roy!

(*Engine coughs again, despite revving.*)

ROY (*defensively*): It's all right, Jenny. Don't fuss me!

JENNY: Is anything wrong with the car?

ROY: No.

JENNY: Roy, mother'll kill me! I promised, I promised faithfully, to be in by eleven o'clock!

ROY: It's only eleven o'clock now.

JENNY: It is not! It's a quarter to twelve.

ROY: All right, all right!

JENNY: And Daddy goes on so in the morning. (*Imitating*) "What *keeps* you out as late as that? What do you *do* all that time? Anybody would think you hadn't *got* a home." And . . . (*The car hesitates and comes to a stop*) Roy, we've stopped! What *is* wrong?

ROY: Look, Jenny. (*Facing it*) We've run out of petrol. (*She does not reply. He goes on in a rush.*) Look, Jenny. I couldn't help it. It was the old man.

JENNY: Oh?

ROY: He must have wanted me to use my own pocket money to get the tank filled. And I never noticed what the gauge was registering. (*Bitterly*) What's more, if you hadn't spent the whole evening dancing with Bill Lucas . . .

JENNY: So it's all *my* fault, is it?

ROY: I didn't say that. I said . . .

JENNY (*sweetly*): And does it matter, Roy Saunders, how many times I choose to dance with Bill Lucas?

ROY: No, it does not!

JENNY: Oh, why can't you ever say anything *nice?*

ROY (*shouting at her*): I'm absolutely crackers about you! Don't you know that?

JENNY (*offhandedly*): No. I don't.

ROY: WELL, I AM!

JENNY: And is *that* your idea of being nice?

ROY (*muttering*): Dancing the whole evening with that . . . that . . . (*Suddenly deflated*) Look, Jenny. I'm sorry.

JENNY: For what?

ROY: For getting you stranded out here.

JENNY (*tentatively*): Roy?

ROY: 'm?

JENNY: It doesn't *really* matter.

ROY: Anyway, it's not as bad as it might be. There's an AA box in the Heathcott Bypass. I know where we are.

JENNY: That's miles from here!

ROY: It is if you go by the road. But I can cut cross-country. You see that stone wall with the bright green moss on it? There's a house beyond it.

JENNY: Couldn't you get some petrol at the house?

ROY: Nobody lives there. It's, well, it's the place where old Mr. Brede used to live. (*Hurriedly*) Now you take it easy! I can walk it in ten minutes, and phone Tom Stanley, and be back in another ten minutes.

JENNY: Roy?

ROY: Well?

JENNY: I don't want to be left alone.

ROY (*hesitating*): You could come with me. But it's going to be a bit rough on your shoes and that dress.

JENNY: I don't care! . . . There are some people, you know, who wouldn't go anywhere near that house.

ROY (*loftily*): *You* don't believe all that eyewash?

JENNY: No, of course not! Don't be silly!

ROY: Neither do I. Besides, I'm not going *into* the house.

JENNY: Where *do* you go?

ROY: Through some gates in the wall and up a drive between trees. (*Pleading*) Look, Jenny; you stay here. I'll only be gone twenty minutes, just twenty minutes, and then Tom Stanley will . . .

JENNY (*suddenly*): Roy, I can't stay here by myself!

ROY: *Are* you coming along, then?

JENNY: Yes. Please!

(*Music up. The next part of the scene on echo.*)

JENNY: What's that funny effect on our voices?

ROY: It's the trees. They meet overhead like a tunnel.

JENNY: Roy, strike a match.

ROY: What for?

JENNY: I can't see anything at all. I'm scared.

ROY (*bursting out*): Now look, Jenny!

JENNY: Please strike a match!

ROY: Okay. Whatever you say! (*Match struck*) Is that better?

JENNY: Nothing but damp leaves underneath. We can't even hear ourselves walk. And if something should step out from behind a tree . . .

ROY: For the love of Mike, come *on!*

JENNY: You're afraid *too.* Aren't you?

ROY (*ignoring this*): We'll be away from the trees in a minute. The drive turns, and we come out practically in front of the dining room windows.

JENNY: Roy, listen.

ROY: Well?

JENNY: I . . . I know the real reason why Mr. Brede shot himself.

ROY (*jumping*): *Ow!* The damn match burnt my fingers!

JENNY: I do so know it! My Uncle Fred is a friend of the doctor who was there. And Uncle Fred says . . .

ROY: Walk slowly. Keep your hand out in front of you.

JENNY: Don't you believe me?

ROY: Mr. Brede was a what-d'ye-call-it—a neurasthenic. His nerves were gone, that's all.

JENNY: Yes, but don't you know why he finally took a gun and . . . (*Pause*) It was because he hadn't slept, not a wink, for twenty nights. And that was because something was after him.

ROY: How do you mean?

JENNY: Mr. Brede was in the house in the middle of the night, and the phone rang. He got up to answer it, and said "Hello" . . . but there wasn't any reply, although he could hear somebody breathing. He said, "Hello, who's there?" and started to shout at it. But still there wasn't any answer, until the other person softly hung up the receiver. And the same thing happened the next night. And the next.

ROY: He didn't *have* to answer the phone, did he?

JENNY: Uncle Fred says . . .

ROY: Uh?

JENNY: Did *you* ever hear a phone ringing in the middle of the night? And wonder and wonder and wonder? That's what Mr. Brede did. And finally he couldn't stop himself. He'd rush at the phone, hoping it *wasn't.* But . . .

ROY (*protesting*): Look, Jenny! I . . .

JENNY: There it was. Just the soft breathing, and the click when the receiver went up. He tried getting other people to answer for him, but it was always an ordinary call. They said, "Have the phone taken out," but he wouldn't do it. Then after a fortnight it started to happen in the daytime. Uncle Fred says his nerves had been all haywire as it was, but when *that* began to happen . . .

ROY (*abruptly*): Why are you stopping?

JENNY: I thought I heard a door close.

ROY (*protesting*): Jenny! Listen to me!

JENNY: It *sounded* like a door.

ROY: There hasn't been anybody in that house for fifteen years.

JENNY: But . . .

ROY: This is where the drive turns. You can see starlight now, and there's the house. And . . .

(*Slight pause.*)

JENNY (*crying out*): Roy! Look there!

(*Music up.*)

SHAW: Go back a little now. Go back a little, please, to the morning of that same day. When people say to me, when they say, "Dr. Shaw, why didn't you prevent it?" I can only tell them I'm not a magician; I couldn't have foreseen. That's why I want you to think now of a very different scene. I want you to think of the seafront promenade at Weyford on a bright July day. . . .

(*We faintly hear under the next speech a band playing "I Do Like to Be Beside the Seaside," which comes up slowly as* SHAW *goes on.*)

SHAW: The blue sky, the yellow sand, the gleaming-headed bathers, the crowds on the promenade, the pier like a white centipede with black legs. Over there, in that little park, the bandstand. On the outer fringe of the bandstand crowd, be pleased to watch that hearty-looking, blue-chinned man sitting on a bench and idly reading a magazine. Look. He glances up from the magazine as . . .

(*The band comes to the end of the piece. There is a distant murmur and a spatter of applause.*)

MARSH: By all that's holy, it's . . . (*Calling*) Colston! Jimmy Colston!

(*Slight pause.* JAMES COLSTON *is about forty, with a thin, intense voice which contrasts with* MARSH'S.)

COLSTON: Good afternoon, Marsh.

MARSH: Here. Sit down on this bench.

COLSTON: Thank you.

MARSH: Are you holidaying here too?

COLSTON: No. I live here.

MARSH: Well! Weyford's all right for a holiday; I'm not saying a word against it, mind; but give me London every time.

COLSTON (*faintly satirical*): Still, even a busy solicitor, I gather, must take time off occasionally?

MARSH: That's right. We all get in a rut, you know. Good air. Good . . . I say, old man. *You're* looking a bit seedy!

COLSTON (*with sudden bitterness*): Are my clothes so *very* unpresentable, then? My hair and nails not attended to every fortnight? My shirt cuffs just a little *too* frayed?

MARSH (*startled and confused*): Listen! Colston! I never meant . . .

COLSTON: Didn't you?

MARSH: I was talking about your health.

COLSTON: I'm perfectly well, thanks.

MARSH: Great Scott, man! (*Tries to laugh*) Far from meaning . . . that is . . . well! They tell me you're becoming known as a great writer.

COLSTON: More praise than halfpennies, I'm afraid.

MARSH: And that reminds me. By George, it's the oddest coincidence you ever heard of! I was just reading a story of yours in this magazine.

COLSTON: Yes, so I noticed.

MARSH (*indulgently*): I suppose it's not a coincidence, really. I saw it on the railway bookstall, and saw your name, and thought, "Well! After all! We must patronize old Jimmy."

COLSTON: Thank you.

MARSH: I don't go in much for these highbrow magazines, old man. But I *can* tell you this: *your* story is thundering good.

COLSTON (*quickly*): You like it?

MARSH: Very much!

COLSTON: You honestly like it?

MARSH (*puzzled*): Yes. Didn't I say so?

(*A subtle change is coming over* COLSTON.)

COLSTON: Then may I inquire, Marsh, why you're cheating yourself of the pleasure you *could* get from it?

MARSH: What's that?

COLSTON: Would you enjoy your dinner if you had to eat it in a London bus? Would you care for a Beethoven concert if you heard it next door to a rivetting machine? Look at that page!

MARSH: What about it?

COLSTON: It's plainly subheaded "A Ghost Story."

MARSH: Well?

COLSTON: Hasn't the reader any duties corresponding to his privileges? You've paid a shilling for that magazine?

MARSH: Yes.

COLSTON: It's yours. You have the right to read it whenever and wherever you like. Granted! But surely, Marsh, an author has rights that the reader is bound to respect?

MARSH: Such as?

COLSTON: The right to his undivided attention. To share that attention—as you're doing—with a band playing imbecile tunes . . . a crowd of surf bathers . . . barking dogs . . . children chasing a beach-ball . . . is like kicking him in the face. (*Suddenly*) By God, it's infamous!

MARSH (*mildly*): See here, old man. You're not well.

COLSTON: Why must you keep harping on that?

MARSH: And aren't you making rather heavy weather over a small point?

COLSTON: You call it a small point?

MARSH: Yes, I'm afraid I do.

COLSTON: Some moods—laughter, or tears, or compassion—you can get anywhere. But the supernatural . . .

MARSH: And what would you call the right surroundings for reading a ghost story?

COLSTON: Night. Solitude. A lonely house and a lighted candle.

MARSH (*expostulating*): Now hang it, old man! I couldn't . . .

COLSTON: I don't say you could. I don't say you would. I only say that's what any honourable—or, if you prefer, sporting-minded—reader would do.

MARSH (*slowly losing his temper*): Sporting-minded, eh?

COLSTON: Yes. That's what I said.

MARSH (*rather contemptuously*): Do you think these "suitable surroundings" would make any difference? (*No reply*) Come on, now! If I read a story of yours under those conditions, do you actually think you could give me the shivers?

Or make my hair stand on end like a man in a comic paper?
Me?

COLSTON (*almost in pity*): My dear Marsh. How little you know!

MARSH: Meaning what?

COLSTON: I have studied fear for twenty years. I have experimented with fear. The late Mr. Charles Brede could tell
you . . .

MARSH: Charles Brede? Who's he?

COLSTON: He was a friend of mine. . . . I have done that,
Marsh, for one purpose. To capture on paper those subtle
forces that mend the soul or destroy it. The slow, fine toil of
getting the words just right. (*Breaking off*) Under the
proper circumstances? You wouldn't dare!

MARSH: Wouldn't I, now!

COLSTON: You haven't the nerve. You're brave enough—oh, yes!—
to read a mild story of mine in a public park, listening to a
band. But alone! At night! In a deserted house! I have a
manuscript in my pocket that would kill you!

MARSH: Look here, Colston. Do you know of any such house?

COLSTON (*slight pause*): You mean . . . ?

MARSH: *Do* you, Colston?

COLSTON: Come to think of it, I do.

MARSH: Take me there tonight.

COLSTON: I see!

MARSH: Leave me your story and a candle. Call for me when I've
had time enough to read it, and I'll tell you the entire plot
and . . . kick you out of the place. Is *that* sporting enough?

COLSTON (*pause*): Yes. (*Starts to laugh softly*) Yes, I think it is.
(*Music up.*)

SHAW: Think, now, of Roy Saunders and Jenny Ames . . . moving with shaky knees up a tree-lined drive at just on midnight. Emerging from that tunnel, merging rather suddenly
almost opposite dusty, half-broken, full-length windows . . .

JENNY (*crying out*): Roy! Look there!

ROY: Sh-h. I see it.

JENNY: What's a light doing in that window?

ROY (*struggling with relief*): It's a candle. Probably tramps,
that's all.

JENNY: Roy! You're not going any closer?

ROY: It's only tramps. They camp out in old houses. I just want to *see*. That's all. I won't make a sound; I promise. (*Fading off*) I just want to . . .

JENNY (*calling softly*): Roy. (*Pause. Jenny mutters to herself.*) You can be very brave, can't you, when you think it's only tramps? And we're still miles from home. And no petrol. And what Daddy'll say tomorrow morning if I don't get home all night . . .

ROY (*guardedly*): Jenny.

JENNY: W-what is it?

ROY: There's a bloke in there. . . .

JENNY: Not . . . ?

ROY: No, not a ghost. A man. And he's no tramp, to judge by his clothes.

JENNY: What's he doing?

ROY: He's sitting at an old table with a kind of . . . batch of papers. Just . . . reading. And he looks . . . funny.

JENNY: How do you mean, funny?

ROY: The veins in his forehead are standing out. His mouth is all twisted up. He's got his hands round the edges of the table, as though . . . (*Distant cry*) It's all right, Jenny. That's only a screech-owl.

JENNY (*shivering*): "Only!" "Only!" "Only!" Roy, please, let's get away from here! Are we going to that AA box, or aren't we?

ROY: Yes. Sure. Of course. Only . . .

JENNY: Which way?

ROY: Round the left side of the house . . . that's it . . . and on to the path here. Look, Jenny, you needn't walk so fast. I was just wondering why that bloke should be . . .

(*Off, a man's scream of mortal terror, followed by the thud of an overturned table.*)

JENNY: What's that?

ROY: It wasn't any screech-owl! Wait a minute!

JENNY: Roy! Come back here! (*Screaming*) Roy!

ROY (*calling, off*): He's fainted, Jenny. The table's upset, and the candle's set fire to those papers. I've got to get in.

JENNY: It's no business of ours!

ROY (*unheeding*): Window stuck . . . no way of . . . stone! That's what I want. A big stone!

JENNY: Roy, we'll get into trouble!

(*Crash of glass.*)

JENNY (*controlling herself*): If I've got to follow you, Roy

Saunders, I'll follow you. But if I ever in my life go out with you again, if I ever as much as *speak* to you again, Roy Saunders, as long as I live . . . (*Abruptly*) I can't see anything. Where are you?

Roy: It's all right. I've got the fire stamped out.

Jenny: I said—where *are* you?

Roy: Inside the room. Stay there until I can light this candle again.

Jenny: You b-bet I'll stay at the window.

Roy: There. Candle lighted. Why don't you come in?

Jenny: The man you saw . . . ?

Roy: He's passed out cold on the floor.

Jenny (*hesitating*): All right. I'll come in. Only . . .

Roy: Mind the broken glass. But you don't need to walk on tiptoe. There's nothing to be afraid of.

Jenny: If there's nothing to be afraid of, why did he give that awful yell? And why is his face such a horrible colour?

Roy: He's fainted, Jenny. Sir! (*Slight pause, then urgently*) Sir! Wake up!

Jenny: We ought to throw water over him. Or give him brandy. Or something. Who is he? What's he doing here?

Roy: Jenny.

Jenny: Well?

Roy (*suddenly scared*): Let's get out of here!

Jenny: Why do you say that *now*?

Roy: Look, Jenny. He hasn't fainted. I think he's—

Jenny: No!

Roy: Yes, I think so.

Jenny (*wildly*): Now you've done it, Roy Saunders!

Roy: I didn't do anything! I never touched him!

Jenny: Then what—?

Roy: Listen! (*Heavy, slow, spaced footfalls on wood, approaching*) There's somebody walking in the passage outside that door!

(*Door opens.*)

Shaw: Don't be alarmed. Hold up that candle, young man, and look at me. Look! Doesn't either of you recognize me?

Jenny: You're—you're Dr. Shaw!

Shaw: That's right, my dear. I know your uncle. But I think . . . yes, I think I've got here too late. Is this man dead?

Roy: *We* didn't kill him!

JENNY: We didn't do *anything!*

SHAW: I know that, my dear. A manuscript killed him.

ROY: A—a what, sir? And what are *you* doing here?

SHAW: Never mind that. The point is: this man . . .

ROY: Who is he, Dr. Shaw?

SHAW: He's a solicitor named Marsh. He made a bet with Mr. Colston that Colston couldn't write a ghost story that would scare him. Please remember that because you may have to testify.

JENNY (*alarmed*): Testify?

ROY (*impressed*): Look, sir. You mean a ghost story could be so bad that a person who read it might die?

SHAW (*sigh*): Yes, I mean just that.

ROY: I wonder what the story was about.

JENNY (*shocked*): Roy!

ROY: And now it's burnt to blazes! They were loose sheets, and the candle caught 'em, and . . .

SHAW: I'd better examine him. (*Slight pause*) Yes. Yes. It's too late, right enough. No pulse. No respiration. We'll just try the watch-glass test to make sure.

ROY: What's that test, sir?

SHAW (*fussed*): Don't get in my way now!

ROY: But what is it?

SHAW: You take a watch—here's his own watch on the floor—and hold the glass close to the patient's lips. If there's the least trace of life—sometimes so faint it doesn't show in the pulse —then this glass will be misted. I put it near his mouth like this. . . .

JENNY (*crying out*): Dr. Shaw! Look!

SHAW (*not loudly*): It is!

ROY: He's still alive?

SHAW: Just alive and no more.

ROY: You mean we're going to hear what the story was about?

SHAW: Confound the story! Young man!

ROY (*eagerly*): Yes, sir?

SHAW: My car's down in the road near yours. Nip down there and get the medicine case out of the back seat. If his heart's in anything like good condition, I can pull him round here and now!

(*The ticking of a heavy clock to indicate passage of time.*

*Then the muttered fighting and thrashing noises of a man
emerging from unconsciousness.*)

SHAW: Steady, Mr. Marsh! Steady!

MARSH (*dazed and terrified*): Keep away from me!

SHAW: Young man.

ROY: Yes, sir?

SHAW: Hold his other shoulder. Tightly! Keep him sitting in the
chair!

MARSH (*dazed*): Candle burning. Same room where . . . (*Rous-
ing*) *Who are you?* You're not Colston! (*Almost screaming*)
Who are you?

SHAW: I'm a doctor.

MARSH: Doctor.

SHAW: I've been—well, attending Mr. Colston for nervous disor-
ders. His housekeeper phoned me late tonight and told me
about this bet of yours . . .

MARSH: Who are these other two?

SHAW: Only a couple of young people. They may have saved
your life when the manuscript caught fire.

JENNY: What happened, Mr. Marsh?

ROY: What was in the manuscript?

MARSH (*grimly*): So you want to know what was in the manuscript?

SHAW: Don't talk. Don't excite yourself.

MARSH: I'm going to talk. I've got to talk. Why? Because Colston
cheated!

SHAW: Cheated?

MARSH: He gave me a sealed packet. He said I wasn't to open it
until five minutes past twelve. Got that? Five minutes past
twelve. And I played fair, curse him. I played fair!

SHAW: Please! If you'd only take it easy. . . .

MARSH (*desperately*): Listen! You other two!

ROY (*engrossed*): Yes, sir?

MARSH: I sat at the table. Watch on one side, sealed packet on
the other. Facing that big window—it's broken now—with
the night outside. It was lonely, you know. Lord, how lonely
it was! But I waited. And at five past twelve—not till then!—
I opened the packet. There was a letter inside the manuscript. I read it and stuck it in my pocket just before . . .

SHAW: Easy, I tell you!

MARSH: I've got it. (*Fumbling*) I'll read it to you.

SHAW: For the last time, Mr. Marsh . . . !

MARSH: Listen. "My dear Marsh," it said, "forgive me for the trick I've played on you."

SHAW: *Trick?*

MARSH: "There's no manuscript, Marsh. It's all blank paper. But I've thought of a better idea."

SHAW: *What's that?*

MARSH: "I am unutterably weary. Weary of poverty, weary of illness, weary at the failure of my life's work. I propose to kill myself, Marsh. I propose to put a bullet through my head just as Charles Brede did, at exactly twelve o'clock tonight. I have promised to call for you. You know me well enough to expect me. But, my friend, *it will be after twelve o'clock.* That's all." (*Pause*) And then, Doctor, a screech-owl called out in the garden. And I glanced up. And there was Colston standing in that window with a bullet hole in his head, looking at me. Don't you believe me, Doctor? *Don't* you believe me? Then look for yourself! *He's outside the window now!*

(JENNY *screams piercingly. Music up.*)

SHAW: As a word of explanation, then, may I read a short press-cutting from the local paper of some three weeks after that date? (*Slight pause*) "Mr. James R. Colston, of Bush Villa, Enfield Road, who is well known for his short stories in the *London Stylus,* was yesterday confined to the Hollymere Asylum for the Dangerously Insane. Mr. Colston, who also confessed to a series of hoax telephone calls which cost the life of the late Charles Brede, was apprehended as the result of his latest experiment in 'the psychology of fear' when he appeared at a window with a painted bullet wound on his forehead. Though he was overpowered by Dr. Daniel Shaw and Mr. Roy Saunders, we learn that it has been necessary to confine him to a strait-jacket. Most of our esteemed contemporary's fellow writers are still at large."

(*Music up.*)

October 12, 1944.

"Death and laughter," Anthony Boucher remarked, "are old friends." Nowhere is that idea better expressed than in the wild humor of Carr's novels about Sir Henry Merrivale. Only a handful of his radio scripts, however, feature hilarious coincidences worthy of P. G. Wodehouse, combined with subtle clues worthy of John Dickson Carr. The best of these is "White Tiger Passage," written for a revival of *Appointment with Fear* in 1955.

White Tiger Passage

THE CHARACTERS:

Bill Stacey	Willie Whiskers of the *Record*
Jenny Holden	His friend
Henri Duchene	Of the *Sûreté*
Malcolm Derwent	Managing Editor of the *Record*
Mavis Derwent	His wife
Harold K. Johnson	Secretary of the Grayson Hotel
Stella	Switchboard operator
Telephone operator	

Setting: Brighton, 1954.

NARRATOR: Brighton. The pleasant town of Brighton in the warm and sunny summer of the year 1954. (*Heavy roll of thunder, followed by splashing rain*) Undoubtedly it is raining in Brighton as it is raining everywhere else. But away from the seafront, in the old and haunted streets called the Minories, the skies are not more bitter than the heart of that young journalist—Bill Stacey of the *Daily Record*—standing there in the street by the telephone box. Unhappy, did I say? Well, he may not be more unhappy than the girl watching him from a distance, both of them unconscious of the pouring rain as . . .

(*Another heavy thunder roll.*)

BILL (*to himself*): I won't do it! I can't take it any longer! There's nothing to do but phone 'em and tell 'em I'm through! It's no good trying to—

JENNY: Please forgive me, but—

BILL (*roused*): I beg your pardon?

JENNY: Please do forgive me, but aren't you . . . ?

BILL (*bitterly formal*): Yes, madam. Yes, I am. Unfortunately, the reward for today has already been won.

JENNY (*puzzled*): The reward?

BILL: Yes, madam. Why don't you repeat the formula? "You are Willie Whiskers of the *Daily Record*, and I hereby claim the *Daily Record*'s prize of five pounds for identifying you." To my shame and sorrow, madam, I *am* Willie Whiskers.

JENNY: But I wasn't going to say that.

BILL (*off balance*): You weren't going to . . . ?

JENNY: No. You're Bill Stacey, aren't you? Don't you even recognize me? I know it's been five years; I know the light's bad, but . . . Jenny Holden?

BILL: Yes, Jenny. Yes, I recognize you.

JENNY: I'm sorry. I shouldn't have spoken to you. . . . Aren't you even glad to see me?

BILL: Of course I'm glad to see you. (*Restraining himself*) I think you know that.

JENNY: Then what was the matter? Why didn't you write to me?

BILL (*bitterly*): I was going to do great things in Fleet Street, wasn't I?

JENNY: You were! You are!

BILL: Ha, ha! I am Willie Whiskers of the *Daily Record*.

JENNY: But—

BILL: How would *you* like to have a name like Willie Whiskers? Or tramp through seaside towns, week after week in the rain, acting like somebody in a cloak-and-dagger spy story, but only leaving cards in toy shops and milk bars?

JENNY: Then show them what you can do! *Make* them give you a better job!

BILL: Ha, ha, ha!

JENNY: And was that why you didn't want to recognize me? Because you think you're a failure?

BILL: "Think" I'm a failure! You don't know my news editor. I interviewed Henri Duchene, the head of the Paris police. And they wouldn't print a word I wrote. They think I'm too impetuous.

JENNY: But if you get them a really big story, wouldn't they be bound to give you a chance?

BILL: No, they wouldn't even let me handle it. I'm on the track of just that same big story: front page and exclusive. If I could only *show* them! (*Rain increases to a roar.* BILL *wakes up vaguely.*) By the way, Jenny. Isn't it raining?

JENNY (*meekly*): Well, yes. It is a bit.

BILL: Then we'd better dive into the telephone box. Anyway I've got to phone my Willie Whiskers story to London. In you go, and there'll be plenty of room for both of us.

(*Folding door opens and closes. Noise of rain blotted.*)

JENNY: Now what *is* this big story? What's it about?

BILL: Murder.

JENNY: *Murder?*

BILL: Yes! Haven't you heard about the Slasher of the Boulevards?

JENNY: No, never! It sounds foreign and—rather nasty.

BILL: Yes, it's both. The Slasher's a lunatic murderer, who's been scaring everybody in Paris for three weeks. I told you, didn't I, that I interviewed the head of the Paris police?

JENNY: Yes. Well?

BILL: His visit to England a week ago was *supposed* to be a holiday. But I didn't believe it. We had lunch at Beltring's. I thought good food and a quiet, solemn atmosphere would get the best results. And then . . .

JENNY: Something went wrong?

BILL: No; but he wasn't exactly suited to the stuffiest restaurant in London. Fat and jovial, all right, but with a big mustache and a thundering foghorn voice, when . . .

(*A small restaurant background has crept in behind the speech. It fades as we hear the voice of* HENRI DUCHENE.)

DUCHENE (*loudly*): And it is only I, old Papa Duchene of the Sûreté, who will tell you the real truth.

BILL: Well, sir?

DUCHENE: You 'ave ask me, young man, what is your greatest English institution. Good; I tell you. It is your limerick.

BILL: Our—what?

DUCHENE (*excitedly*): Limerick, limerick! You 'ave not 'eard of 'er? Listen! (*Very loudly*) "*There was a young lady from Brighton, Whose skirt was a terribly tight 'un—*" (*A very large plate drops and smashes.*) Cré nom, but what is the matter?

BILL: Didn't you see the waiter drop the serving dish and the meat with it? I'll bet *that's* never happened here before!

DUCHENE: He do not like my limerick? But she is one very funny limerick.

BILL: She may be, sir. But she'll play the devil if you shout her out in Beltring's restaurant!

DUCHENE (*gleefully*): Aha, and now I understand. It is again the English hypocrisy, yes?

BILL (*firing up*): Now just a minute, Monsieur Duchene! I'm getting pretty damn sick and tired of hearing nothing but your remarks about English hypocrisy! Do you think it takes any courage or intelligence just to shout limericks in public?

DUCHENE (*sneering*): But *you* would not do it? Eh?

BILL: You think I wouldn't?

DUCHENE: I know it!

BILL: Then *you* listen! (*Blaring*) "There was a young lady from China—" (*Very heavy crash of about a dozen plates*) Oh, I say! I oughtn't to have said that! I— (*Angrily*) What's so very funny *now*?

DUCHENE (*chuckling*): Young man, I like you. Shake 'ands!

BILL: Certainly! But what . . . ?

DUCHENE: You think I am one old buffoon, eh? Wit'out the taste or the manners? But no! Once upon a time I, Papa Duchene, was myself a *journaliste*. Now I give you a little test. And then—by golly, I like you. (*Blandly*) So I tell you what you really want to know.

BILL (*guessing*): What I really want to know about—?

DUCHENE: About the Slasher of the Boulevards. I am 'ere in England to arrest 'im.

BILL (*startled*): To *arrest* the Slasher?

DUCHENE: *Bien sûr.* In his own home.

BILL: You're not saying this Paris Slasher is really an Englishman?

DUCHENE: And why not?

BILL (*worried*): It could be, of course . . .

DUCHENE: It is! Attend to me, my friend. This person is not normal. He is mad, and he have a madman's logic. Does he wish to commit his little murders and rip up victims wit' a sharp knife? *Bien.* Then he goes to Paris wit' a logic, and he return as meek as milk. (*Grimly*) But he will not be meek, I think, when Papa Duchene has come to arrest him.

BILL: What does Scotland Yard say about all this?

DUCHENE (*loftily*): Your coppers? I don' know. I have not trouble to consult them.

BILL: But you can't make an arrest in England without the cooperation of the English police. Besides, suppose something happens to you? Don't you keep notes? A notebook?

DUCHENE (*lofty conceit*): And am I, Duchene, to write notes of what I can much better keep in my head?

BILL: But that pencil clipped to your breast pocket—?

DUCHENE: Ah, the pencil. No, no, no! Always I keep her to make doodles or write limericks on the tablecloth; that is all. And I warn you, my friend! You will not print one word of what I say now—

BILL (*protesting*): Listen, sir! It's—

DUCHENE: —or I will not give you the exclusive story when I capture the Slasher in twenty-four hours. Furthermore, you will not follow me today or try to play detective yourself. You promise?

BILL (*struggling*): I say, sir; I think—

DUCHENE: No promise, no story! You will not try to play detective? Understood?

BILL: All right; I promise. But if I had just *one* clue to this Slasher . . . !

DUCHENE (*chuckling*): Alas, alas! Then you have not pass my little test after all.

BILL: What part of the test?

DUCHENE: To see if you are a good newsman, of course. For I have already told you the clue, my friend. I have already told you the clue.

(*Music up.*)

BILL: —consequently, Jenny, I'm no nearer to the truth in this ruddy telephone box than I was a week ago. You know, I liked old Duchene. He had a monumental conceit and a weird sense of humour, but I liked him. That was the last time I saw him alive.

JENNY: *Alive?* You don't mean he's . . . ?

BILL: Look, Jenny, where have you been for the past week?

JENNY: I've been on holiday in Brussels. I haven't even seen an English newspaper.

BILL: Duchene came down here to Brighton on the evening of the same day.

JENNY: To Brighton?

BILL: Yes. That was the clue he gave me in the limerick: he was going to Brighton. Only I was too thick-headed to see it then.

JENNY: And—afterwards?

BILL: Well, late that night, Duchene's body was found in a little street called White Tiger Passage, not fifty yards from here. He hadn't been robbed, but the pencil he always carried was missing. He'd been first stabbed in the back, and then . . . well, disembowelled.

JENNY (*fear rising*): Bill! Don't you think—?

BILL (*unheeding*): I told the police what I knew. And they didn't believe me, or said they didn't. I told my news editor, and went over his head to the managing editor; and they let a "more experienced man" cover the story. And the Slasher may be prowling round this phone box now!

JENNY: Bill, haven't you—haven't you got to phone the office with your Willie Whiskers account?

BILL: *Willie Whiskers!* (*Wearily*) Yes, I suppose I'd better.

JENNY: After all, Bill, is it so *very* terrible an assignment to be Willie Whiskers?

BILL (*sharply*): What do you mean?

JENNY: Well! When you think of all the horrible and dangerous assignments they *might* give you . . .

BILL: I see. (*Defeated*) Then you, my darling, won't back me up either.

JENNY (*electrified*): *What did you call me?*

BILL: Never mind. It doesn't make any difference. I think, for a toll call from here, you just dial "o" and the operator gets the number.

(*Phone is picked up. One complete twirl of the dial, then the ringing tone which continues steadily under the next speeches.*)

BILL (*half-muttering*): And yet, you know, I might have solved the whole thing. I had a theory. Only nobody would listen.

JENNY (*mood changed; yearning*): I'll listen to you, Bill. Tell me!

BILL (*bitterly*): What difference does it make now? You said . . .

JENNY: It does make a difference, my dear. It makes every difference! Tell me your theory and we'll *both* go after the murderer.

BILL (*staggered*): But only a minute ago you said . . .

JENNY: Oh, never mind what I said! Darling, this is the most important thing in the world!

BILL: One day, by the Lord Harry, I am going to understand women! Until then—

JENNY: Tell me! Please!

BILL: Well, *I* maintain Duchene wasn't killed in White Tiger

Passage at all. *I* say he was killed somewhere else, and his body carried there.

JENNY: Why do you say that?

BILL: Why should he first have been stabbed in the back? Why was that pencil missing? Because the murderer crept up to him while he was hanging about somewhere, waiting maybe, and making idle scrawls with the pencil. The trouble is, it's too wide a field! Where *could* a man have been standing with his back turned, making idle scrawls, while he . . . while he . . .

(*Ringing tone ceases.*)

OPERATOR (*on filter*): Operator. Can I help you?

BILL (*suddenly inspired*): Got it! While he was waiting for a telephone call to be . . . *Jenny!*

OPERATOR (*sharply*): *Operator! Can I help you?*

BILL: Operator, dear, you've helped me already. Thanks a million! Goodbye! (*Phone slammed down.*) *Jenny!*

JENNY: Bill, have you gone off your head?

BILL: Look here! On the shelf beside the phone.

JENNY: But it's only a lot of scrawled names and phone numbers. I know lots of people who . . .

BILL: Yes, but look where I'm pointing. Just under the capital letters "M.D."

JENNY: It's a phone number. 7-0-3-1. That seems familiar somehow. But . . . wait! I've just come back from Belgium; and there's—

BILL: Yes, there's a line drawn across the center of the seven. All people from France or the Continent write a seven like that. And just underneath the number—look!

JENNY (*slowly*): "There was a young lady from Brighton . . ."

BILL: Jenny, we've got him! The Slasher of the Boulevards! I'll give you ten to one that his initials are M.D. and his phone number is 7-0-3-1. (*Wildly*) Where's that phone?

(*Phone lifted. Full twirl of dial.*)

JENNY (*alarmed*): Bill! You're not going to ring that number straightaway?

BILL: You'll see what I'm going to do, my dear. You'll see.

(*Music up.*)

STELLA (*on filter*): Central double o, double o.

BILL: *Daily Record?* Is that you, Stella?

STELLA: It certainly is, Mr. Stacey. And at the top of my form. You want extension 4-6, don't you?

BILL: No, not this time. Put me straight through to the managing editor.

STELLA (*horrified*): Mr. Derwent?

BILL: Yes. He says he's always glad to encourage his staff. And this is real news!

STELLA: I wouldn't do it; honest I wouldn't! He's in an awful temper; Maisie Griggs says he's been having more trouble with his wife. I could let you speak to his secretary.

BILL: No. This is too important! Mr. Derwent's private office. Please, Stella. Be a good girl.

STELLA: We-ell . . .

BILL: You'll do it for me, won't you?

STELLA: Righty-ho. But they'll kill me if they ever find out. Just a moment.

JENNY (*furious*): Who *is* this Stella?

BILL: Never mind! She's just a girl. Sh-h. Quiet!

DERWENT (*on filter*): Yes? Yes? Malcolm Derwent here. What is it?

BILL: Listen, Mr. Derwent. This is Bill Stacey speaking. . . .

DERWENT: Oh, no! *No!* Not you *again?*

BILL: I couldn't help it, Mr. Derwent. I've got real news!

DERWENT: Then why the hell don't you speak to the news editor. Why do you have to keep pestering me?

BILL: Because you're the only one who can give me permission to cover it. It's murder; it's front page . . .

DERWENT (*tone changing slightly*): Are you with the police now?

BILL: No. The police don't know anything about it.

DERWENT (*gritting his teeth*): Then do you think we'd be allowed to print a word of it? (*Very virtuously*) Never forget, Stacey, that we are good citizens even before we are newspapermen. Your duty is to go straight to the police with any . . . (*Sharply*) Stop a bit! Where are you phoning from?

BILL: Brighton.

DERWENT: Brighton? This isn't the Henri Duchene story, is it?

BILL: Yes! And I've got the murderer's telephone number and practically his name!

DERWENT: I see. I see. Now never forget, Stacey, that often we can be of much more assistance to the police if we do a little investigation beforehand. I want you to know that all of us here at the *Record* appreciate your—your enthusiasm and your desire to serve. (*Heartily*) You deserve a reward for this, and I'm going to give it to you.

BILL (*jubilant whisper*): You hear that, Jenny? (*Back to phone*) Thanks, Mr. Derwent. I can't tell you how I thank you!

DERWENT: Not at all, my boy, not at all. It's the least I can do.

BILL: Right, sir! Any instructions?

DERWENT (*businesslike*): Yes. Now we'll send an experienced man to Brighton as fast as a car can take him. You tell him what you've got; he'll deal with it, of course. (*Benevolently*) As for you, Stacey, you may forget your Willie Whiskers story for the rest of the day! How's that?

BILL (*pause*): And this is the reward you were going to give me?

DERWENT: Of course. What else can you expect? (*Pause*) Are you still there, Stacey? Can you hear me?

BILL: Yes, Mr. Derwent. Can *you* hear *me*?

DERWENT: Yes, of course.

BILL: You're *sure* you can hear me perfectly?

DERWENT: Yes! Yes!

BILL (*exploding*): Then to hell with Willie Whiskers, to hell with the *Daily Record*, to hell with you and all your ideas of a reward!

DERWENT: Young man, are you sober?

BILL: Yes, worse luck! All I wanted was a chance, and you'll never give me one, will you? All right! Either I handle this story, myself in person, or I go straight to the police as you said I ought to do. What do you say to that?

DERWENT (*bursting out*): I say . . . (*Correcting himself to a stealthy and sinister tone*) Very well, Stacey. You wanted your chance, and you shall have it.

BILL: What's the catch in *this*?

DERWENT: There's no catch. You will bring me the full story behind the Duchene murder before we go to press tonight. Do that, and I'll put you on crime reporting. Fail to do it, Mr. William Stacey, and you will not even be Willie Whiskers or anyone else connected with this newspaper! *Is that clear*?

BILL: Well, I . . .

JENNY (*furious*): Bill, give me that phone!

BILL: But . . .

JENNY: Yes, Mr. Derwent, that's quite clear! And what's more, he'll do it!

DERWENT (*taken aback*): Who the devil's that?

JENNY: This is Miss Jennifer Holden, Mr. Stacey's secretary and assistant. And do you want to know what I think of you, Mr. Derwent? *Blaah!*
(*Phone violently banged down.*)

BILL (*worried*): Well, Jenny, there's nothing like ticking off the boss to promote good relations at the office.

JENNY: You'll get the story! I'm certain you will!

BILL: You know, you put so much life and soul into me that . . . well, I'll tell you later. But—yes! I can do it! With you there, I can get the old swine any story he wants!

JENNY (*meek again*): I—I'm awfully glad I can help you, Bill. Because I'm afraid we're rather in the soup. I've just remembered the address of the telephone number. 7-0-3-1 is the number of a hotel.

BILL: Oh, crikey. There goes my job!

JENNY: No, no, it's not as bad as you think. Grayson's is a residential hotel, very high priced and stuffy and Regency, run by the same people as Beltring's. Its guests are permanent guests. If your idea is right, the Slasher is certain to be there. But you can't just ring up the hotel and say, "Look, have you got a murderer staying there?"

BILL (*inspired again*): Oh, yes, you can, if you go about it the right way. And I think I know how! (*Phone picked up*) 7 . . . 0 . . . 3 . . . 1 (*Ringing tone*) You see what happened to old Duchene, don't you?

JENNY: No. Why should he have been killed in this phone box? And why should the murderer have taken his body somewhere else?

BILL: Because—for some reason—he knew Duchene was here and followed him. The Slasher couldn't tell who Duchene might have been calling; Duchene might have given the whole game away with his call. The Slasher stopped him with a knife. Then he thought he had to get the body away, in case the call should be traced and somebody would remember seeing him here.

JENNY: But you can't trace a call from a public box.

BILL: I know that, but lots of people think you can.
(*Ringing stops. Click of phone picked up at other end.*)

MAVIS (*on filter*): Grayson's Hotel.

BILL (*becoming the stuffy official*): Good afternoon, madam.

MAVIS (*suddenly lyrical*): Good afternoon, good afternoon, good afternoon! And isn't it a *lovely* afternoon in the early evening?

BILL (*taken aback*): I beg your pardon?

MAVIS: Granted! And you have *such* an attractive voice. Why don't you come over and have tea with me?

BILL: I can't help feeling, madam, there must be some mistake. But I wish more switchboard operators were like you.

JENNY (*fierce whisper*): Bill Stacey, this is the absolute end! Must you make improper advances to every woman you meet?

BILL (*incautiously loudly*): But I'm not making improper advances!

MAVIS: Aren't you? What a pity! As a matter of fact, I'm not the switchboard operator. I'm a guest. But whenever this mouldy old foyer is empty, I've longed and longed to sit down and make rude remarks to anyone who rings up. But I can't make rude remarks to *you*, my pet. Who are you?

BILL: Hem! My name is Stacey, madam. I'm the assistant station master at the railway station. Will you be good enough to tell me whether there is anyone at Grayson's Hotel with the initials M.D.?

MAVIS (*slight pause, then sharply*): Is this a joke or something?

BILL: No, madam, certainly not. But many of our passengers forget things and leave them in the train. Now this suitcase I have here . . .

MAVIS: Suitcase?

BILL: It's a very handsome suitcase; dark blue leather; locked; might be a man's or a woman's. But the only identification is a cardboard label attached to the handle, with the initials M.D. and the address of Grayson's Hotel.

MAVIS (*lyrical again*): Oh, how nice! How interesting and mystery-making! But, you see, there are two people with those initials.

BILL: Two people?

MAVIS: Yes. And how delightful! One of them is me.

JENNY (*fierce whisper*): Bill! Don't you remember the limerick? "There was a *young lady* from Brighton." And that woman—

BILL: Quiet! She'll hear you!

MAVIS: The other person is Mark Dawley. *Dr.* Mark Dawley. All the old ladies here—ugh!—think it's terribly comical to speak of Mark Dawley, M.D.

BILL (*sudden suspicion*): A doctor? Is he also a surgeon?

MAVIS: I really don't know, but he's so jumpy and nervous I shouldn't like to have him operate on *me*. And he's just come back from a long continental visit with Mr. Johnson, so I expect the suitcase is his.

BILL (*whispering*): And Jack the Ripper was supposed to have been an insane surgeon!

JENNY (*whispering*): It's that woman, I tell you!

MAVIS: Really, you know, *I* can't remember leaving a suitcase in a train. But then I'm so horribly forgetful. I'll tell you what, though. You come over here immediately with the suitcase. And I'll have tea ready—of course I mean cocktails —and we can be nice and cozy while we look at it.

BILL (*loudly*): Madam, I'm afraid that's impossible! My duties here—

MAVIS (*claws showing*): Now don't be horrid to me, my pet, or I'll ring up your station master and make a *dreadful* complaint about you.

BILL: I mean, madam, I can't possibly be there straightaway.

JENNY (*under her breath, bitterly*): No. We've got to buy a suitcase first.

MAVIS: Then mind you come as soon as you can; I'll count on it. Oh, dear, there's old Miss Kittredge doddering across the foyer to spy on me. I'm afraid I've got to ring off. Good—

BILL: Wait! Just a moment! You haven't told me your name.

MAVIS: Oh, of course. (*Laughing*) How stupid of me! I'm Mavis Derwent. My husband is the editor of the *Daily Record*, and he'll be so amused when he comes down here tonight. Goodbye, angel. Goodbye.

(*Music up.*)

NARRATOR: It was a long time before Bill could keep his promise. Due to a long argument as to the right kind of suitcase and its contents, it was fully an hour and a half before the two conspirators entered the stately portals of Grayson's Hotel. In the lofty, dimly lit foyer they found nobody more alarming than a plump, bald-headed gentleman, affable but worried, in a morning coat of irreproachable cut.

JOHNSON: Forgive me, my dear sir. (*Doubtful*) I imagine you are—er—the assistant station master?

BILL: Certainly. And why shouldn't I be?

JOHNSON: No reason, no reason. Though I had fancied, from your appearance . . .

BILL (*very official*): And who, sir, might you be?

JOHNSON: My name is Johnson, Mr. Stacey. I'm the secretary here.

JENNY: Whose secretary, please?

JOHNSON (*benevolently*): Between ourselves, Miss—Mrs.—

JENNY: I am Mrs. William Stacey, thank you.

JOHNSON: Ah! I applaud your husband's caution. Between ourselves, "secretary" is an old-fashioned and fancy term for manager. I flatter myself I'm a little more than that, as director of several enterprises like this. Still! I'm proud of our fine old traditions, and even a managing director doesn't object to acting as secretary and father-confessor. (*Earnestly*) That is why, Mr. Stacey, I most earnestly implore you not to go up to Mrs. Derwent's suite at this time.

BILL: And why not?

JOHNSON: Unfortunately, her husband has just arrived.

BILL (*appalled*): Her husband?

JOHNSON: It would appear that one of our oldest and most valued guests, Miss Honoria Kittredge, elected to phone Mr. Derwent and inform him—no doubt with good reason—that his wife had made an illicit appointment with the assistant station master. Mr. Derwent, being a man of somewhat choleric temper, immediately jumped into his car . . .

JENNY: Bill, you've *got* to go up there!

BILL: Jenny, don't be ridiculous! (*Correcting himself*) The fact is, sir, we're convinced this bag belongs to Dr. Mark Dawley. Is the doctor in, by any chance?

JOHNSON: Yes, I believe so. But he's in one of his moods today—temperament, you know—and . . . oh, very well! I'll take you to his room. If you will please come this way?

JENNY (*uneasy*): Mr. Johnson, what did you mean by saying Dr. Dawley is in one of his moods?

JOHNSON (*tolerantly*): Well! The doctor has a large and I believe valuable collection of surgical knives. When he decides to clean and sharpen them, he is—distraught. But he will be very cheerful, I am sure. Into the lift, please.

(*The creaking of a folding inner lift-door, then the opening and closing of the door itself.*)

JOHNSON: This is the top floor. Turn to the right, please, and follow me.

JENNY: But this doesn't look like a hotel corridor.

JOHNSON: Didn't I tell you, dear lady, that Dr. Dawley has peculiar tastes? I shall just take the liberty of opening the door . . . (*Door opens.*) After you, Mrs. Stacey. After you, dear sir. Thank you. (*Door swiftly closed. Key turned in lock.*)

JENNY (*terror rising*): This isn't a hotel room at all. And why did you lock that door?

JOHNSON: For the same reason, my dear, that I now firmly grasp your arm.

JENNY: *Bill!*

JOHNSON: No, young man! You will stand very far back. This knife I have here is a very interesting knife. I have only to press the button . . . (*sharp click*) . . . and a double-edged blade springs out. And now, Mr. William Stacey of the *Daily Record*, you will tell me everything you know about the Slasher of the Boulevards.

BILL: I don't know anything! I was only coming here to find out!

JOHNSON: You expect me to believe that? What did Duchene really tell you at Beltring's restaurant?

BILL: Nothing important, I swear!

JOHNSON (*heavily satirical*): You didn't know, even though I tested you by suggesting it, that the letters M.D. stand for "managing director"? You didn't know, even when Mrs. Derwent told you on the phone, that I've recently returned from a long visit to the Continent with Dr. Dawley? You didn't know that this hotel is under the same management as Beltring's restaurant?

BILL (*realizing*): Then you were there! And saw me with Duchene! You followed him here and killed him!

JOHNSON: Yes. And you didn't know that, I suppose?

BILL: No! I thought the murderer was Dr. Dawley. But I know it now, because you've just confessed to murder in front of two witnesses.

JOHNSON: You . . . never . . . suspected . . . ?

BILL: Never! And you've given yourself away.

JOHNSON: I think, young man, that a long and deep slash through your wife's coat . . .

JENNY: Bill! There's somebody outside this door!

(*Fusillade of quick, heavy knocks on the door.*)

BILL: Jenny! Tear away from him! Get behind me! That's it! Now, Mr. Slasher Johnson, would you like to take a cut at *me* with another witness outside the door?

DERWENT (*muffled but raging*): Who's in there? I know you're there! I can hear you!

JENNY (*low voice*): Isn't that Mr. Derwent?

BILL (*low voice*): Yes, he would be here. And it's a flimsy door. If I can just make him furious enough . . .

DERWENT: Miss Kittredge saw the man with the suitcase get into the lift, and somebody press the button for the top floor. Who's in there?

BILL (*yelling*): I'm in here, old boy! The man with the suitcase! How's your wife?

DERWENT: *Who are you?*

BILL: Never mind who I am. Why don't you come in and get me?

DERWENT: You think I can't break down this door?

BILL: I know you can't, you old windbag!

(*A series of frantic kicks with a shoe continue heavily, and cease just as* JENNY *speaks.*)

JENNY: Bill! Look out! The knife!

BILL: Yes, and I've got the suitcase for him too. Take it, Slasher!

(*Noise of a leather object coming into violent contact with somebody's head and face. A cry and a body falling.*)

BILL: You see, Jenny, how much better it was to fill that thing with bricks instead of women's clothes? He's knocked cold!

(*Battering at door begins again. Door bangs open.*)

DERWENT: Where's the man who made love to my wife? Where's the man . . . Oh, no! *No!* Not you *again?*

BILL: Look on the floor, Mr. Derwent. That is the Slasher of the Boulevards!

DERWENT: I will strangle you with my own— What did you say?

BILL: I tell you Johnson is the Slasher! He confessed to Duchene's murder in front of Jenny and me. Look at his knife there; it's still got dried blood on it. I've got the story, and I can prove it!

DERWENT (*sharply*): Is this true?

BILL: Yes, sir. But I never made any improper advances to your wife. I never—

DERWENT (*sharply*): Stacey!

BILL: Sir?

DERWENT: Stop talking like a fool and run downstairs to a phone! This story will carry your byline, and the police are bound to let us use it because *we* got it! My dear boy, what are a few improper advances against a scoop like this? Run, Stacey, run!

JENNY: Oh, dear! And this is Fleet Street!

(*Music up.*)

August 2, 1955.

PREFACE TO
The Villa of the Damned

In his first detective story, John Dickson Carr explained how a person can disappear from a closely guarded room, and in his later stories and novels people vanish from swimming pools and telephone booths. He could also make weapons, money, and an entire apartment disappear. The impossible situation in "The Villa of the Damned" may be the most daring of all. It is surely incredible that an entire suburb—and perhaps an entire century—can vanish like smoke. . . .

The Villa of the Damned

THE CHARACTERS:

Brenda Stannard	The wife
Alan Stannard	The husband
Angela Stannard	His sister
Bianca da Carpi	A woman with a reputation
Pietro Rossi	A man who catches stones
Septimus Goodlaw	An Anglican clergyman
Railway guard	
American tourist	

Setting: Rome and Naples at the time of Mussolini.

NARRATOR: Our story takes us back more than fifteen years. When I tell you that at this time young Alan Stannard was very wealthy, was about to stand for Parliament, was perhaps too much immersed in history, you may be apt to consider him something of a stuffed shirt. You would be wrong. Any such tendency had already disappeared under the influence of Brenda Stannard, the girl Alan had just married. And so, as we follow these two on their honeymoon in Italy, we hope we shall keep our promise to bring you *An Appointment with Fear!* Naples, 1937. But here, I fear, we see no romantic background, no blue water along the bay, or Vesuvius purple in a heat haze. Instead we see the gloomy, grimy cavern of the railway station, where a large, green-painted express train seems forever on the point of leaving for Rome. Brenda and Alan Stannard, holding hands, stand at one compartment window. . . .

(*Great bustle and slamming of train doors.*)

RAILWAY GUARD (*shouting in agony*): *Presto tempo! Il traino departite! Presto tempo!*

ALAN: I can't keep on saying, "Do you love me?"—

BRENDA (*quickly*): Darling, why not? *I* don't mind.

ALAN: So I'll merely ask, how do you like Italy?

BRENDA: It's wonderful! But *why* must they make such a dreadful fuss and uproar just about getting the train started?

ALAN: This is one of Il Duce's trains. Notoriously, in the press anyway, they always start on time.

GUARD (*growing hysterical*): *Il Traino departite!* Oh, *Corpo di Bacco—*!

BRENDA: The guard is having a fit. The people on the platform are beginning to dance. There's a woman flying along with her hat over one eye and her . . . (*Breaking off, astonished*) Alan! I think it's your sister!

ALAN: But it can't be! Angela's gone to Capri.

(ANGELA *is a little feather-headed; incoherent in her meanings though not in her speech.*)

ANGELA (*calling breathlessly*): Alan! Brenda! Wait!

ALAN: By George, it *is* Angela!

ANGELA: Oh, dear. I ran and ran and ran, and I thought I should be *miles* too late!

ALAN: It's all right, Angela. We haven't even moved yet.

ANGELA: Oh, dear, I'm *so* forgetful. I forgot to give you your nice present.

ALAN (*surprised*): A hundred English cigarettes! They're hard to find here; in Naples at least. Angela, I can't thank you enough.

ANGELA: *Silly!* They're not a present from *me*. They're from a very dear friend of mine. And you *must* call on her in Rome.

ALAN: Of course; glad to. Who is she?

ANGELA: I keep telling you. She's a very dear friend of mine, though of course I only met her for a few hours in London. And you mustn't mind if she's terribly, terribly religious, and has a clergyman there most of the time.

BRENDA: Isn't that rather extreme? In keeping sin at bay?

ANGELA: Brenda! I didn't mean religious in *that* way. She's beautiful and blond, and *very* fascinating. You mustn't let Alan see her too often.

ALAN: Who *is* this friend of yours? What's her name?

ANGELA: Bianca da Carpi.

ALAN (*rather startled*): Bianca da Carpi?

BRENDA (*suspicious*): You sound as though you *did* know her.

ALAN: No, I've never met her. But I've read a good deal about her family history. Daggers, poison, and treachery for more than five hundred years.

BRENDA: Please, Alan. I don't really like that kind of talk.

ALAN (*absorbed*): But you can't deny it has a certain sort of fascination. Bianca da Carpi owned—or did own—a villa outside Rome. It's not much more than three centuries old, but it's supposed to be badly and malignantly haunted. Angela, does this lady speak English?

ANGELA: But I've been trying to tell you. She *is* English.

BRENDA: Oh?

ANGELA: And that villa of hers! It's a *lovely* villa beyond the Aventine Hill, though they've built a horrible new suburb straight up to it. But there was a most unpleasant murder there three hundred years ago or something.

ALAN: Yes, I know.

ANGELA: And Bianca's all dreamy about it, and wrapped up in it, and positively *foolish!* I want to warn you!

ALAN: Warn me? Of what?

ANGELA: You mustn't let her persuade you to . . . Oh, dear!
(*Loud blowing of whistles. Heavy chug of engine getting underway and the grind of wheels.*)

ALAN (*calling*): What did you say? I mustn't let her persuade . . . what?
(*Train moving; sounds growing a little louder.*)

GUARD (*in ecstasy*): Il traino! Il traino!

AMERICAN VOICE: Look, brother. I don't want to butt in, see—

GUARD: *Il traino*— (*Breaking off*) You spikka da Eenglish? You American? Whatta you want?

AMERICAN: Strictly between ourselves, Captain, *did* that train pull out on time?

GUARD (*dramatically*): Sh-h!

AMERICAN: What in Sam Hill d'ye mean, "Sh-h"?

GUARD (*conspiratorial triumph*): Da engine driver, he's a-push his watch back twenty meenoots. So is all a-right, eh?
(*Shouting*) Viva Il Duce! Il traino departite!
(*Train whistle. Train noise comes up and fades.*)

NARRATOR: Rome in lazy summer. In the midst of modern Rome there stand the ruins of that ancient city which once ruled the world. Sometimes under a hot sun its broken pillars and arches are completely silent, all but deserted. But it is towards twilight now, and two familiar figures are trudging up an incline inside the ruin of the Coliseum itself. It is a broad stone passage, but almost dark, when . . .

(*Rattle of small stones as though dislodged by foot.*)

BRENDA: Can't we go out on the gallery?

ALAN: For a last look, then. Give me your hand, and it's only half a dozen steps more. (*Sound of steps on stone*) Here, this is the entrance. Don't be afraid of falling. There's a stone balustrade round the gallery, and they've put up iron railings where the masonry's crumbled. (*Hesitating*) No, stop a bit. I'll lead you.

BRENDA: Then it isn't safe?

ALAN: Oh, the gallery's safe enough. But it's getting dark, and we've got to clear out soon. Here, turn to the left, and along beside the balustrade to . . . here. Now look down.

(*Slight pause.*)

BRENDA: It's so—lonely, isn't it? Horribly lonely!

ALAN: Yes.

BRENDA: And much larger than I ever imagined the Coliseum.

ALAN: A gladiator down there would look as small as a toy soldier. I wonder! (*Stops abruptly*)

BRENDA: Wonder—what?

ALAN: I wonder if that's why all the dead and gone spectators were so greedy for bloodshed. Because they couldn't see it closely. Because it looked like dolls fighting. (*Trying to be jocular*) And I also wonder, Brenda, whether I could stir up any ghosts.

BRENDA (*not alarmed; rather sharply*): Oh? How?

ALAN: Suppose I chucked a stone out there, and threw as far as I could? Let's try it! (*Heavy pebble strikes against stone, bounces as though down rough stone slope, rolls, and noise fades away.*) There! That must have bounced as far as the arena. According to all the rules, I ought to get a reply. The roar of a lion, maybe, or steel clashing. *"Morituri te salutamus!"* But there's no answer, you see. None at all!

BRENDA (*repressed*): Tell me, Alan. Where did you get this sudden obsession about ghosts?

ALAN (*trying lightness; not succeeding*): Oh, I don't know. Old books and hobbies, I suppose; influence of Italy; anything you like.

BRENDA (*quietly*): Then tell me something else. Did you send a message to that woman today?

(*Slight pause.*)

ALAN: What woman?

BRENDA: *Oh, at least don't lie to me!* (*Controlling herself*) You know the woman I mean. This Signora da Carpi, the beautiful widow with the villa. *Did* you send a message to her?

ALAN (*firmly, yet hint of evasion*): No, I did not—

BRENDA (*repressed*): I'm glad.

ALAN: Now look here, Brenda. If you think the da Carpi woman means anything to me, or that I've ever set eyes on her, you're wrong! All I did, here, was imagine things and chuck a stone over the parapet. Like *this* stone! . . . You don't understand, but I can explain in two seconds. The whole thing was caused by— (*Stops abruptly; pause; then alert*) Stop a bit! That's damned funny!

BRENDA: And what is so—so very funny?

ALAN: That last stone I threw. It didn't land anywhere. There was no sound.

BRENDA: No. Come to think of it, there wasn't. (*Impatient*) Well, it probably fell into the sand. Or earth. Or we simply didn't hear it fall.

ALAN: There isn't any sand or earth. And the whole Coliseum is as quiet as a tomb.

BRENDA: Oh, why bother about it?

ALAN: Because there's a very odd game going on. I didn't want to tell you, but something or somebody has been following us all day. . . . Now that last stone: I didn't even throw it; I just flipped it. It must have fallen into the gallery below this one.

BRENDA (*alarmed*): You're not going to climb down there?

ALAN: I don't need to climb down. I can go by the gallery entrance underneath this.

BRENDA: Most of the galleries are wrecked or gone completely! There's an iron bar across the entrances. And it's nearly dark; you'll kill yourself if you fall!

ALAN: Not if I'm careful.

BRENDA: Alan! Please!

ALAN: Now you stay here; I'm just within call. Stay here, and I can be back in two minutes.

BRENDA: Alan! *Alan!*

(*Music up.*)

ALAN (*muttering to himself*): *Must* have fallen in this gallery.

Must have! . . . Easy, son; you'll be over the edge. Must have landed . . . landed . . .

PIETRO: Just about—*here,* signore? Where I am sitting? Yes?

ALAN (*sharply*): Who's there? Who are you?

PIETRO (*humbly*): I am only Pietro, signore. Poor Pietro, fat Pietro. I doff my hat: *ecco* there are holes in it. Yet a man of more ability than my poor clothes might show. Shall I prove myself your friend?

ALAN (*meeting his mood*): Certainly, if you like.

PIETRO: Then take my electric torch—come; take it. I have another. . . . Or you and your good lady will never get out of here tonight.

ALAN: Thank you. I do need it. When shall I return it?

PIETRO (*tranquilly*): You need not. I shall call for it at the proper time.

ALAN: Are you trying to sound like Mephistopheles?

PIETRO: Perhaps I *am* the devil, in a sense.

ALAN (*polite impatience*): If you'll forgive me, Signor Pietro, I'm looking for . . .

PIETRO: A stone, yes? Here it is. I caught it.

ALAN: You caught it? Why?

PIETRO: I think perhaps you are the sort of young man—impetuous, do I say?—who will rush to seek it. (*As though shrugging*) If not—well! There are many other ways I may speak to you alone when your wife is not there.

ALAN: Are you by any chance the man who's been following us all day?

PIETRO (*humbly*): *Scusatemi.* Yes.

ALAN: Now look here!

PIETRO (*alert again*): Softly, young man, softly. Your voice down. The lady above must not hear our words, as I have heard yours. I have done you one favour—yes?

ALAN: Yes. Granted.

PIETRO: I can do you another, believe me, if you will answer a question. And if you will not—*pardon*—become all English and say this is none of my business.

ALAN: Fire away, then! What's your question?

PIETRO: This morning at Hotel Patinello you have received a letter from the Signora da Carpi?

ALAN: Yes, I did.

PIETRO (*almost lyrical*): And was it a large beautiful letter, with monogram as well as crest, and so delicately perfumed?

ALAN: Have you seen this letter?

PIETRO: Only the outside, alas. (*Sharply*) But I guess, eh, what is in the letter?

ALAN: All right, try.

PIETRO: This so pious lady, with her Church of England parson in attendance, has heard from your sister of your interest in the dead. If you would try an experiment this night, if you would see Duke Nicolo himself rise stabbed from his grave, you must come to the Villa da Carpi. A car will call at your hotel at ten o'clock tonight. But you must not bring your wife; you must not even tell her, else it would frighten the poor young lady. . . .

ALAN (*suddenly*): Wait a minute! Do you think my wife noticed that letter?

PIETRO (*pitying him*): Oh, my poor friend! A large letter, monogrammed and perfumed; and a woman does *not* notice it?

ALAN: But Brenda didn't say anything. She didn't say a word at the time.

PIETRO (*giving him up, groaning*): Oh, *Corpo di Bacco!*

ALAN: Stop acting like a pitying Mephistopheles! What is it?

PIETRO: Signor Stannard, you have not long been married. No?

ALAN: No; only six weeks. But—

PIETRO: Do you think any woman, when she is hurt, will at once speak out? A woman, she not say—she think; she brood; inside her the fury grows and grows and grows. And then, when you least expect it—BOOM! However! All this you will learn. (*Insistently*) But you *will* go to the Villa da Carpi tonight. Yes?

ALAN: Yes, I'd certainly intended to. And the da Carpi woman is right; it *would* have scared Brenda.

PIETRO (*soft excitement*): *Bene! Bene!* Good! I congratulate you. This is very wise. But you will not take your wife!

ALAN: I most certainly will, now! Either Brenda goes, or I don't go myself! Haven't there been enough misunderstandings already? I'll explain the whole thing to Brenda.

PIETRO (*fiercely*): You will not be warned?

ALAN: Against what?

PIETRO: I can't—say.

ALAN: Then I can't agree.

PIETRO (*bitter quietness*): As you please. (*Then sardonically*)
But permit me, signore, to change one word of the Latin
quotation I heard you give. "*Mortui te salutamus!*"

ALAN: "*Mortui*"?

PIETRO: "We *who have already died* salute you!" Good night.
(*Music up.*)

NARRATOR: Of course at the Patinello Hotel there was a recon-
ciliation. And Brenda wept; and Alan swore; and both fervently said—it has perhaps occurred to one or two others—
that never again should there be a misunderstanding. And
yet, at ten o'clock when they entered the long limousine,
with its silent driver, they felt . . . not frightened, perhaps.
But uneasy. On edge. They guessed what would happen at
the villa—or did they? (*Traffic noises increase in background.*) Far beyond the Aventine Hill, they were driven
through a noisy new suburb to the villa itself. But there was
nobody to meet them. The door of the villa stood wide
open. It showed them a polished marble corridor running to
the back, with another corridor crossing it in the middle.
Immediately to their left, in the corridor, they could see the
half-open door of a lighted room whose long windows faced
the front. Embarrassed, hesitating, our adventurers shuffled
forward. When they could catch a glimpse of a book-lined
room, and a short, stout, grizzled clergyman . . .

GOODLAW (*worried*): One tries to do one's duty, dear lady. But
my duties are nearing an end. . . .

BRENDA: Listen, there's someone in here.

ALAN: Sh-h.

GOODLAW: . . . You will not accept advice, either from the
Church or from a friend. To take a practical consideration . . .
(BIANCA DA CARPI *is about thirty, a languorous charmer with
much appeal.*)

BIANCA: Practical considerations, Mr. Goodlaw, have always
bored me.

GOODLAW (*wryly*): Yes. I had observed it.

BIANCA: Give me adventure, Padre! (*Quoting with intensity*)
"From the hag and the hungry goblin, that into rags would
rend ye . . ."

GOODLAW (*faint humour*): You quote, as I trust you know, from
Tom o'Bedlam?

BIANCA (*sharply*): Bedlam? Do you suggest a comparison?

GOODLAW: No. Only common sense. If you venture into a waterfront slum at night, in any city in the world, you're in danger of being robbed or killed. Agreed?

BIANCA: Oh, agreed. But it might be amusing.

GOODLAW: It is the same, believe me, in the realm of the spirit. You will find undesirables *there,* forever lurking. And if you deliberately call up evil forces . . . !

BIANCA: I have called them up. Duke Nicolo will be here before midnight.

BRENDA (*whispering*): Hadn't we better go in? Alan?

ALAN (*whispering*): No! Wait! Listen!

GOODLAW (*pleading*): A second consideration, then. Your heart will not stand these "experiments." How many times has Dr. Salvatore warned you?

BIANCA: *Dear* Dr. Salvatore.

GOODLAW: He is a specialist; he knows. If your heart were to give way . . .

BIANCA: Even that might be almost amusing.

GOODLAW: As a last consideration, then . . .

BIANCA (*politely defiant*): Yes, Mr. Goodlaw?

GOODLAW: You imperil your soul. I forbid it!

BIANCA: Really, Padre. (*Laughs*) You are much concerned with my soul, I know. But you must have been aware of my love affairs. Have you ever scolded me so terribly? Or in your heart been so very shocked?

GOODLAW (*quietly*): No honest priest, signora, is ever shocked. He knows too much of human nature. (*Faint despair*) Preaching has never been my forte. I hoped, God help me, it was a phase that would go. But when you propose a love affair with a man who has been dead for three hundred years . . . !

BRENDA (*whispering, too loudly*): Alan! Did you hear that?

BIANCA (*sharply*): Just a moment, Padre. Isn't there someone outside the door?

(*Through the next speeches, we hear a faint clamour of traffic as through open front windows.*)

ALAN (*amiably*): I'm afraid *I* was outside, Signora da Carpi. There was nobody to announce us, so we simply walked in. You don't mind?

BIANCA (*enthusiastic and over-sweet*): But of course I don't mind! How very, very delightf . . . (*Hesitates and changes tone only a little before going on*) And who, may I ask, is this?

ALAN: Signora da Carpi . . . my wife.

BIANCA (*slight pause*): Oh. I see. Yes. May I present the Reverend Septimus Goodlaw?

GOODLAW (*harassed*): Your servant, madam. Yours, sir.

BRENDA: You see, signora, I positively insisted that Alan should take me with him tonight. (*Sweetly*) I hope it doesn't upset your plans?

BIANCA (*over-sweet and gushing*): But not at all, my dear! Quite to the contrary! You see, *he* may like two of us here when he taps on the window.

BRENDA (*bewildered*): He?

BIANCA: Yes, dear. Look at the portrait above the mantelpiece. That is the wicked Duke Nicolo da Carpi at the age of thirty, when Rembrandt painted him in 1635. It's a handsome face, don't you think? And most attractive?

BRENDA: It's a cruel face.

BIANCA: But naturally, my dear. That's a part of the . . . Forgive me. No! I must not mention such things before such an innocent. Your husband will understand. However! When Duke Nicolo died, two years after the picture was painted . . .

BRENDA (*insatiably curious*): How did he die?

ALAN: He was hacked to death by the daggers of his own servants.

BRENDA: Not—in this room?

BIANCA: No, my dear. If you will turn round and look at the windows facing the front— (*Breaking off, revolted, not loudly*) God, that suburb! That filthy, painted stucco. And the noise, the yapping, endless noise!

GOODLAW: Shall I close the windows, signora? And draw the curtains?

BIANCA (*real charm*): Would you be good enough, Padre?

BRENDA: But you were saying, signora?

ALAN (*under his breath*): Gently, my dear. This is only a nonsensical legend.

BRENDA: You were saying, signora?

BIANCA: In Duke Nicolo's time, of course, those suburbs consisted only of open fields with a mud path going through them towards a forest. They caught him there before he could draw his sword or dagger. They left him for dead: only a stained bundle of clothes. But in my dearest friend, my sweetest Duke, there was a power of will greater than life. He crawled forward along the path towards those windows. If only he could enter the house and reach the talisman . . .

ALAN: What talisman? I've never heard of a talisman.

BIANCA: Patience: You will. If he could find the talisman, this luck charm which had so often saved his life, he felt he might still live. He reached the middle window there. He stood up. He scratched at the glass. There he fell dead.

ALAN (*curtly*): If you don't mind, we'll stop upsetting my wife with all this. A straight question, signora: Have you ever seen this Duke Nicolo in the house?

BIANCA (*intent*): No. Never.

ALAN: Outside the house, then?

BIANCA: I—don't know. But sometimes, at twilight . . . yes! I am sure I've seen him!

ALAN: Where?

BIANCA: Outside the middle window. Pressed against the glass. With his white face and the dagger wound through one eye. (*Sharp noise.*)

BRENDA: *What was that?*

GOODLAW (*off*): Forgive me, Mrs. Stannard; I was only closing the curtains on the middle window. Red velvet can seem so heavy. As for the other windows . . .

ALAN: Why are you so sure, Signora da Carpi, his ghost will come in here tonight?

BIANCA (*suppressed triumph*): Because I have found the talisman. The real, original talisman! Ricardo, of the Piazza del Popolo, searched all Europe before he found it. This afternoon there will be certain rites. Oh, Nicolo will be here! Now come with me.

BRENDA: Where?

BIANCA: No matter. All of you. Come with me!

(*Music up.*)

NARRATOR: Strange, wasn't it? Yet it was Alan Stannard who told me this story. He says that, as they turned left in that marble corridor, then left again into the other crossways corridor of the villa, there was a door on each of four sides. But mark this! They never once went outside the villa. Instead, they descended indoor stairs into a damp cellar where the only light was from his own electric torch. Signora da Carpi, speaking no word, opened an ancient bureau and took something out. He could not see what it was; she kept it concealed in her hand. But at that instant, for no apparent reason, fear and confusion seized him like hands round his neck. It seemed to him that he could not see Brenda. Only afterwards when they were back upstairs, amid the twistings of the corridor, and he saw on his left the familiar lighted library, with its red curtains and its walls of books . . .

BIANCA: There, you see? It wasn't a long journey, was it?

ALAN: If nobody else will ask the question, then I will. Signora, what is concealed in your hand?

BIANCA: Only a gold coin, a heavy gold coin. It is polished now, but it was minted more than a hundred years before Nicolo's time by the House of Borgia.

BRENDA: Is that the—talisman?

BIANCA: Yes! (*Coin spins and rattles on wood.*) Will you come for it, Duke Nicolo?

GOODLAW: For the last time, I forbid this! Already in this room there is something . . .

ALAN: Yes! You're right!

BIANCA: The wind is freshening outside; no more.

ALAN: That may be, but there's no other sound from outside! Not a noise in all that suburb!

BRENDA: Well, they—they go to bed early, that's all.

ALAN: But they can't shut off every traffic noise in an instant. Signora! Do you mind if I open the curtains of the middle window?

BIANCA: Not at all. (*In ecstasy*) Open them!

ALAN: No trams. No taxi horns. No voices. Not even . . . (*Sound of curtains flung back. Faint noise of wind outside.*) . . . not even a street lamp. It's the dark of the moon. I can't see anything!

BRENDA: But the light's streaming out from that window. You must see *something!*

ALAN: Yes! There's . . . (*Sharp clash of curtains closing*) God almighty!

BRENDA (*crying out*): *What is it?*

ALAN: I don't want you to think I'm off my head. But—there aren't any houses!

GOODLAW (*steadily*): What *did* you see, young man?

ALAN: Open fields. And a mud path leading towards the forest. And . . .

GOODLAW: Go on. (*Moving off*) I must see this myself. What else was there?

ALAN (*impatiently*): Oh, only a bundle of clothes in the path. Somebody must have . . . (*Suddenly realizing*) *Bundle of clothes!*

BRENDA: Don't open those curtains!

GOODLAW: I will not, madam. I am only peering through them. But your bundle of clothes, young man, is getting up. It is crawling towards these windows.

BIANCA (*crying out*): You have waited too long, Nicolo! Enter!

GOODLAW: Thou shalt not be afraid for the terror by night, nor for the arrow that flieth by day, nor for the pestilence that walketh in darkness, nor for . . .
  (*Three sharp taps on window.*)

BRENDA: Padre! Can't you do something more than . . . ?

BIANCA: *Enter! Nicolo! En—* (*She ends in a bewildered gasp and choke.*)
  (*Heavy coin slides off wood to floor. Sound of falling body.*)

ALAN: What's the matter with her?

GOODLAW (*steadily*): Stand back, everybody. Stand back, if you please. (*Slight pause*) A thousand times she has been warned.

ALAN: Her heart?

GOODLAW: Yes. She has gone, leaving only all the indiscreet letters to shock even Rome. (*Voice rising*) Now she is dead! As dead as . . .
  (*Three more taps on the window.*)

ALAN (*furious*): Who *is* outside there? I'm going to see!

GOODLAW: The Cross of God between us and harm! Stand back!

ALAN: I'm not going to stand back, thanks! I think this is a fake. Whoever, or whatever, is out there, I challenge you! Come in!
  (*Loud and rushing blast of wind as window flies open; flapping of curtains; wind dies away.*)

PIETRO: Good evening, Signor Stannard. I salute you.

ALAN (*bewildered*): Pietro!

PIETRO (*mocking*): Poor Pietro! Fat Pietro! I have come, as I promised, for my torch.

ALAN (*angry*): Like Satan?

PIETRO: Yes, in one sense. For assuredly, like Satan, I catch sinners. (*Sharply and abruptly*) Permit me, signore! I am Commander Rossi of the Italian Civil Police.

ALAN (*startled*): *Police!* You?

PIETRO: That is not flattering, signore. In the meantime, Signora Bianca da Carpi, you will kindly get up from the floor and stop pretending to be dead. As for you, Mr. Goodlaw, who have never been a clergyman in your entire life . . .

ALAN: What the devil is all this about?

PIETRO: About a swindle, Signor Stannard, which has been practised too many times by this pair. If you had come here, as I begged you to do, without your wife, we should have got the complete evidence against them. Even as it is, I think we have enough.

ALAN: Was it you who kept rapping on that window?

PIETRO: Only the second time. The first time it was a fellow conspirator, their servant, who ran away when he saw me and my men. Still, this "Duke Nicolo" was never intended to enter the room.

ALAN: But how could they swindle anybody just by staging a fake ghost appearance?

PIETRO: Ah! That is the beauty! Now tell me: when our gracious lady dropped dead, what was the first question you asked this so pious clergyman?

ALAN: I asked if she had heart failure.

PIETRO: *Bene!* And how did you know of this supposed heart condition?

ALAN: Because Brenda and I heard . . .

PIETRO: You heard everything when you first arrived, as you were meant to hear it. Now again, when the lady apparently died, what else did this good man say to you?

ALAN: I don't know. Something about a scandal.

PIETRO: *Bravissimo!* You are wealthy, yes? You would enter politics, yes? Then suppose you come here alone; the lady dies of a heart attack. But this signora is known over all Rome as of—shall we say?—not good reputation. The good parson cries out that there will be a great scandal, unless much— very much—money is used to bribe the police and hush it up.

Does your wife not already suspect you? If you protest that you were merely looking for a ghost, the roar of ridicule will never leave you. You would have paid, my friend Stannard. Believe me, you would have paid.

ALAN: But I did bring Brenda. Then why . . . ?

PIETRO: Why did they go through with it? I wonder.

GOODLAW (*cynically*): Then let me tell you. My dear Bianca's love of playing a part, any part! Anywhere!

BIANCA: Shut up, you fool! They can't prove it. Let them try to prove it!

GOODLAW (*tolerantly*): As for me, my dear, I am tired of ministering, in the literal sense, to your hysterics. What a damn sort of life a real parson must lead!

BRENDA: But, Signor Rossi . . .

PIETRO: At your deepest service, Signora Stannard.

BRENDA: These people may be swindlers, but they aren't magicians. They can't make a whole suburb disappear and put open fields in its place.

PIETRO (*rather impatiently*): Come, signora, that was the easiest of all. Both you and your husband can tell us how.

ALAN: No! I'm hanged if *I* can!

PIETRO: Listen to me. When you went to the cellar you went out of the library and turned to the left. You entered the crossways corridor and also turned to the left. Then you went downstairs. When you returned, therefore, *any* turning must have been to the right?

ALAN: Yes. Naturally.

PIETRO: And yet, if you think back, you still saw the library door on the left. Am I correct?

BRENDA: You mean they simply took us to another room? Decorated exactly like the first? But this room is at the back. And with its windows . . . ?

PIETRO: Its windows, of course, looking out on the open fields you always knew were there. (*Triumphantly*) I explain miracles, signora! Behold! I am again—Mephistopheles!
(*Music up.*)

August 23, 1955.

JOHN DICKSON CARR was one of the most popular, acclaimed, and influential writers of the mystery novel's "Golden Age." His specialty was the locked-room mystery, and he developed two classic detectives who were adept at solving these apparently impossible crimes: Dr. Gideon Fell and (in books written under the pseudonym "Carter Dickson") Sir Henry Merrivale. Among his many novels are *The Three Coffins, The Arabian Nights Murder, The Blind Barber, The White Priory Murders, The Judas Window, The Skeleton in the Clock,* and *The Burning Court.* He was also the author of a biography of Sir Arthur Conan Doyle, and over seventy-five radio scripts for both the BBC and American radio. The Mystery Writers of America presented him with their Grand Master Award for his lifetime achievement in detective fiction.